Noel Goodey   Diana Goodey   Karen Thompson

Messages

Workbook

1

My name is ....

I am in Class ....

The name of my school is ....

My English teacher is ....

My address is ....

....

....

Date ....

CAMBRIDGE
UNIVERSITY PRESS

What do you remember?

1 Word work

Nouns

a Look at the pictures and write the words.

b Put the words into three groups.

 1

 2

 3

Animals

dog _____

_____

_____

gdo ___ *dog* ___   tca _____   palpe _____

 4

 5

 6

Food

_____

_____

_____

zipza _____   agb _____   kobotone _____

In the classroom

_____

_____

_____

 7

 8

 9

nnaaab _____   keds _____   palethne _____

2 Write about you

Complete the sentences.

I'm _____
_____

I like _____
_____
_____

I've got _____
_____
_____
_____

3 What's the reply?

Match sentences 1–6 with the replies (a–f).

1 What's your name?
2 How are you?
3 Do you understand?
4 What is it?
5 Goodbye.
6 Hi! I'm Paulo.

a Hello. I'm Carmen.

b Yes.

c It's an elephant.

d Goodbye. See you tomorrow.

e Anita.

f I'm fine, thank you.

1 _e_   2 ____   3 ____   4 ____   5 ____   6 ____

4 Punctuation

Write the sentences. Use capital letters and the correct punctuation.

1 howareyou   _How are you?_

2 i'mfinethanks   _____

3 myname'sroberto   _____

4 whatisit   _____

5 it'sanapple   _____

6 ilikeanimals   _____

5 Days of the week

Complete the puzzle with days of the week. Then write the days in order in the diary.

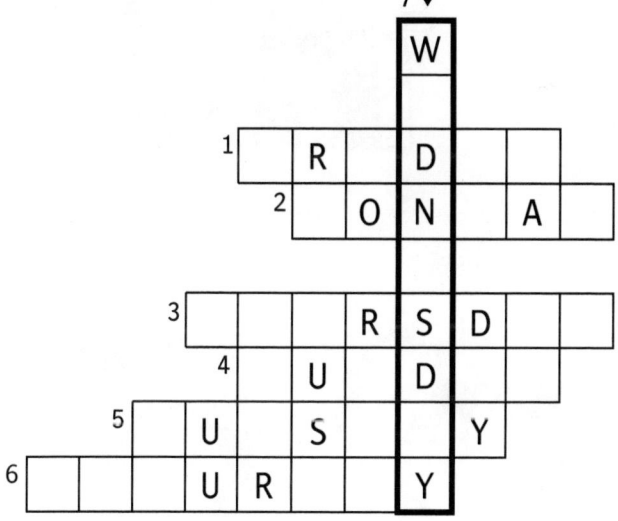

September

6 Monday
7
8
9

10
11
12

6 Extension *Find more words*

Look again at Exercise 1. Add some more words to the three groups.

Animals: _____

Food: _____

In the classroom: _____

1 Classroom language

Match the pictures with the sentences in the box. Write the sentences under the pictures.

> What does it mean?   Can you help me, please?   I know.
> Pardon? Can you say that again?   I don't know.

4 ....

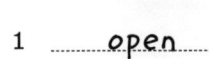

1 ....

2 ....

3 ....

5 ....

2 Word work *Verbs*

Put the letters in the right order and make verbs. Write the verbs under the pictures.

> drea   ~~pone~~ ska   kolo   rewans   stilen   sleco   twire

1 ....*open*....

2 ....

3 ....

4 ....

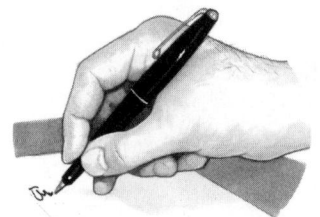

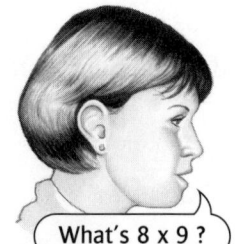

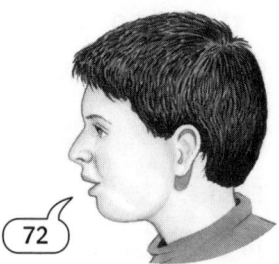

5 ....

6 ....

7 ....

8 ....

4   Module 1

3 Classroom instructions

Make eight instructions. Use the verbs in box A and choose nouns from box B.

A ~~write~~ open close look at read listen to
ask make

B a friend the CD the pictures your dictionary
your book the board the sentences a list
the song ~~a letter~~

1 Write a letter.

2 _____

3 _____

4 _____

5 _____

6 _____

7 _____

8 _____

4 he/she and his/her (G) 1a, 21c

Complete the sentences. Use *He's, She's, His* or *Her*.

1 His name's Joe.
_____ fourteen.

2 _____ name's
Sadie. She's twelve.

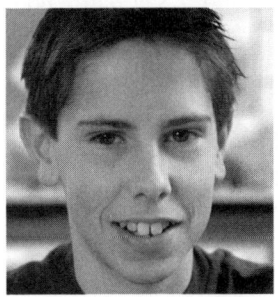

3 _____ name's
Jack. He's thirteen.

4 Her name's Kate.
_____ eighteen.

5 What's the reply?

Complete the conversation. Circle the right reply: a, b or c.

1 HELEN: Hi! I'm Helen.
  ELISA: _____
  a I don't know.
  (b) Hi!
  c Hi! I'm 13.

2 HELEN: What's your name?
  ELISA: _____
  a Your name's Elisa.
  b No.
  c Elisa.

3 HELEN: What nationality are you?
  ELISA: _____
  a Spain.
  b She's Spanish.
  c I'm Spanish.

4 HELEN: Where do you live?
  ELISA: _____
  a In Malaga.
  b In Spanish.
  c You live in Malaga.

5 HELEN: How old are you?
  ELISA: _____
  a Don't panic!
  b Yes, I'm fine.
  c I'm thirteen.

6 Extension *Who is it?*

Look at the information about Joe, Sadie, Kate and Jack in the Student's Book (pages 8 and 9). Write the correct names.

1 __Jack__: I live next door to Sadie.

2 _____: I'm 12.

3 _____ and _____:
We like computers.

4 _____: I've got two sisters.

5 _____: I'm at university.

6 _____: Sadie's my friend.

7 _____: I'm 18.

8 _____: I'm 14.

1 Numbers

Match the words in A with the words in B and make sentences.

A		B	
1	My friend Joe is	a	0 eight 0 seven nine three six double four two.
2	My telephone number is	b	double 0 seven.
3	We live	c	ninety-four.
4	Look at page	d	at number eighteen.
5	James Bond is	e	~~fourteen~~.

1 _e_ 2 _____ 3 _____ 4 _____ 5 _____

2 Ordinal numbers

Write the numbers. Use the words in the box.

third	tenth	second	eighth	~~first~~	fifth
fourth	sixth	ninth	seventh		

1st ____first____   6th _____

2nd _____   7th _____

3rd _____   8th _____

4th _____   9th _____

5th _____   10th _____

3 The alphabet

Say the letters. Write the odd one out in each group.

1 D F B E _____ _F_

2 H K J Y _____

3 S L C M _____

4 U Q I W _____

5 A T P V _____

6 N X R F _____

4 Listening *Letters and numbers*

Listen to the letters and numbers.
Tick (✓) the right answer: a or b.

1 a 13 ✓   b 30 _____

2 a T _____   b D _____

3 a 40 _____   b 14 _____

4 a M _____   b N _____

5 a 80 _____   b 18 _____

6 a V _____   b W _____

Can I open the window?

5 Asking for permission and for help

Put the words in the right order. Make three questions asking for permission and two questions asking for help.

1 window / open / can / the / I ?

Can I open the window? _____

2 I / letter / your / can / read ?

_____

3 look / your / I / at / photos / can ?

_____

4 do / how / 'Liverpool' / spell / you ?

_____

5 you / how / English / 'carne' / say / in / do ?

_____

6 Extension *A secret message*

Do you understand the code? What does the message say?

C N O E T E I D W

A I P N H W N O

_____ ?

Unit 1 Learning diary

Date _____

In Unit 1 I revised:

	Easy	Not bad	Difficult
words I remember from primary school.	☐	☐	☐

desk, bag, pizza, _____

things I can say about myself.	☐	☐	☐

My name's _____ . I'm _____ .
I live _____ . I've got _____ .

how to say and write the date in English.	☐	☐	☐

It's the first of September.   _1st September_ _____
It's the second of October.   _____
It's the third of November.   _____
It's the fourth of December.   _____

classroom language.	☐	☐	☐

I don't know.   = _____ (in my language)
I don't understand.   = _____
What does it mean?   = _____
Pardon? Can you say that again? = _____
Can you help me, please?   = _____
Can I use your dictionary?   = _____
How do you spell it?   = _____
How do you say that in English? = _____

saying hello and goodbye in English.	☐	☐	☐

Hello. How _____ you? I'm _____ .
Goodbye. See you _____ .

Unit 1 was

interesting ☐   quite interesting ☐   not very interesting ☐

2 Are you ready?

1 Key vocabulary *Members of a band*

Complete the questions about Joe's band. Write the words in the puzzle.

A: Who's the ¹_____?   B: Joe Kelly.
A: Who's the ²_____?   B: Mel Adams.
A: Who are the ³_____?   B: Barney Sutton and Lee Harper.
A: Who's the ⁴_____?   B: Sadie Kelly.
A: What's the band ⁵_____?   B: Monsoon.
A: Are the ⁶_____ of the band students?   B: Yes, they are.

Now look at number 7. Who is it? _____

2 *be*: short forms (G) 2a

What does Carlo say? Rewrite the sentences. Use the short forms *'s, 'm* or *'re*.

1 I am a basketball player.
2 My name is Carlo Madeo.
3 Adriana is my girlfriend.
4 She is a tennis player.
5 We are at university in the USA.
6 She is from Vibo and I am from Palmi.
7 They are places in southwest Italy.

1 *I'm a basketball player.*
2 _____
_____
3 _____
_____
4 _____
_____
5 _____
_____
6 _____
_____
7 _____
_____

3 *he/she/it/they* (G) 1a, 2a

Correct the sentences about Joe's band. Change the underlined words to *He, She, It* or *They* and complete the sentences.

1 The members of the band are at university.

No. *They're* at *school* .

2 The band is called Mushy.

No. _____ called _____ .

3 Mel is the leader of the band.

No. _____ the _____ .

4 Lee and Barney are the keyboard players.

No. _____ the _____ .

5 Sadie is the singer.

No. _____ the _____ .

6 Joe is the drummer.

No. _____ the _____ .

4 Personal information

Read the information about Mel and complete her sentences. Use the short forms 'm or 's.

Name: Melanie
Surname: Adams
Age: 14
Nationality: English
School: Westover School, Exeter

My name ___'s___ Melanie, but my friends call me _____ .

I _____ fourteen.

I _____ English.

I _____ a _____ at Westover School.

It _____ in _____ .

Now write about you.

Name: _____
Surname: _____
Age: _____
Nationality: _____
School: _____

My name _____ .

I _____ . I _____ .

I _____ at _____ .
(Name of your school)

It _____ in _____ .

5 Wh- questions G→14

Complete the questions with Who, What, Where, When or How. Then match the questions with the answers.

1 ___What___ 's your name?

2 _____ are you, Carmen?

3 _____ nationality are you?

4 _____ are you from?

5 _____ 's the girl in this photo?

6 _____ 's your birthday?

a She's my English pen friend.
b Barcelona.
c I'm OK, thanks.
d I'm Spanish.
e It's tomorrow.
f Carmen.

1 __f__ 2 ____ 3 ____
4 ____ 5 ____ 6 ____

6 Extension *Write a conversation*

Complete the telephone conversation with the words in the picture. Use the right punctuation.

greatweneedanothersingerinthebandcometothenextpractice
whenisittsomorrowwhereisitinroom12okseeyououttomorrow
Obimasingergreat...class10bimasingeriminuminclass10bimasingerimin
nameshelenyesmy
shesmynameladams
hatmeladamshelloist

HELEN: Hello. _____

MEL: Yes. _____

HELEN: _____

MEL: Great. _____

HELEN: _____

MEL: _____

HELEN: _____

MEL: _____

HELEN: OK. _____

Unit 2   9

1 Questions on the dialogue

Look at the conversation between Sadie and Jack on page 16 in the Student's Book. Circle the right answer: a, b or c.

1 Where are they?
   a On the beach.
   b At the bus stop.
   c At school.

2 Who's in the photo?
   a Annie and her brother.
   b Annie and her boyfriend.
   c Annie and her cousin.

3 Who's good at sport?
   a Annie and Jack.
   b Mark and Annie.
   c Mark and Jack.

4 Sydney is ...
   a the capital of Australia.
   b a city in Australia.
   c a city in England.

2 *be*: affirmative and negative G→ 2a, 2b

Complete the sentences.
Use *'m, 'm not, 's, isn't, 're, are* or *aren't*.

1 Jack _____*isn't*_____ good
   at sport.

2 Jack _____ very good
   at geography.

3 Sadie _____ at the bus
   stop with Jack.

4 Mark and Annie _____
   at Westover School.

5 They _____ Australian.

6 I _____ Australian.
   I _____ _____ .
   (your nationality)

7 Mark and Annie _____
   brother and sister

3 *be*: questions G→ 2c, 2e

Put the words in the right order and make questions.

1 in / are / a / band / you ?
   Are you in a band?

2 Westover / friends / your / at / are / School ?
   _____

3 your / they / class / are / in ?
   _____

4 he / English / your / is / teacher ?
   _____

5 am / Group 1 / in / Group 2 / or / I ?
   _____

6 late / are / we ?
   _____

7 Liverpool / Australia / in / is ?
   _____

8 it / is / England / in ?
   _____

4 Listening *Find the mistakes*

Listen to the four students. Underline the wrong sentences and correct them.

1 Justin is from Jamaica. He's 13. He isn't very good at sport.
   He's very good at sport.

2 Emma is from Australia. She's 12. She's good at music.
   _____

3 Dan is Australian. He's 15. He's interested in animals.
   _____

4 Martha and Mike are American. They're 14. They aren't interested in computers.
   _____
   _____

5 Key vocabulary *Interests and activities*

Complete the words for interests and activities. Use the letters in the box. Then write the activities in order, with your favourite at the top.

| sic | mming | ding | uter | rt | ames | ~~ort~~ | ience | king |

1 sp _ort_   5 comp_____ g_____
2 sc_____   6 a_____
3 mu_____   7 swi_____
4 coo_____   8 rea_____

6 *be*: short answers  2c

Complete the questions and write the short answers.

1 _____**Is**_____ Sadie interested in music?
Yes, she is._____

2 _____ Jack good at geography?
_____

3 _____ you brilliant at maths?
_____

4 _____ you and your friends all thirteen?
_____

5 _____ Annie and Mark brother and sister?
_____

6 _____ Sadie and Jack cousins?
_____

7 _____ Manchester the capital of England?
_____

8 _____ Buenos Aires the capital of Argentina?
_____

7 *and* or *but*?

Complete the sentences. Use *and* or *but*.

1 Barney is in the band _____**but**_____ he isn't the leader.
2 Joe is in the band _____ he's the leader.
3 Canberra is in Australia _____ it's the capital.
4 Sydney is in Australia _____ it isn't the capital.
5 I'm good at football _____ I'm not good at tennis.
6 I'm not bad at music _____ I'm interested in Bach.

My order of preference

☺ 1 _____
  2 _____
  3 _____
  4 _____
  5 _____
  6 _____
  7 _____
☹ 8 _____

8 *very good at / quite good at ...*

Look at Jack's marks. Write sentences. Use *very good at, quite good at, not bad at* or *not very good at.*

Jack Ellis

Science	85%
Art	65%
Music	40%
French	57%
English	91%

1 **He's very good at** _____ science.
2 _____ art.
3 _____ music.
4 _____ French.
5 _____ English.

9 Extension *Are you good at science?*

Write about you. Use *very good at, quite good at, not bad at* or *not very good at.*

I _____ science.
I _____ music.
I _____ art.
I _____ English.

1 Key vocabulary *Geography*

Complete the sentences. Use the plural form of the words in the box.

~~city~~   mountain   volcano   country   river   lake

1 Toronto and Beijing are _____cities_____ .

2 The Nile and the Thames are _____ .

3 Everest and Kilimanjaro are _____ .

4 Vesuvius and Popocatepetl are _____ .

5 Greece and France are _____ .

6 Titicaca and Victoria are _____ .

2 Reading *Sydney*

Read the text and complete the sentences. Use *is, isn't, are* or *aren't*.

1 Canberra and Sydney _____ cities in Australia.

2 Sydney _____ in the southwest of Australia.

3 Canberra _____ the capital of Australia.

4 The population of Sydney _____ 320,000.

5 Bondi Beach and the Opera House _____ in Canberra.

6 If you _____ interested in surfing, music and fantastic

   food, Sydney _____ the city for you.

3 Extension *Your city*

Write about your city or a city in your country. Use words from Exercise 2.

_____

_____

_____

_____

_____

_____

_____

_____

Learn English in Sydney!

SYDNEY is a city in the southeast of Australia. It isn't the capital. Canberra is the capital, but 3.5 million people live in Sydney and only 320,000 people live in Canberra.

If you're good at surfing, go to Bondi Beach. If you're interested in music, go to the Opera House. And if you're interested in food, Australian food is fantastic.

And remember! Australians speak English. So, come and practise your English in Sydney!

Unit 2 Learning diary

Date _____

At the end of Unit 2 I can:

	Easy	Not bad	Difficult
describe the members of a band.	☐	☐	☐

He's the keyboard player. She's _____ .

use the verb *be*.   ☐   ☐   ☐

I'm _____	I'm not _____
He _____	He _____
She _____	She _____
It _____	It _____

We _____	We _____
You _____	You _____
They _____	They _____

ask and answer questions.   ☐   ☐   ☐

Are you English?   Yes, I am.   No, I'm not.

_____ he Japanese?   Yes, he _____ .   No, he _____ .

Where are they?   _____ in Room 12.

talk about interests and activities.   ☐   ☐   ☐

I'm good at _____ . I'm interested in _____ .

talk about countries and cities.   ☐   ☐   ☐

The capital of my country is _____ .

_____ is a river in my country.   _____ are famous mountains.

KEY WORDS

Members of a band	Interests, activities, school subjects		Geography	
lead guitarist	cooking	_____	country	_____
_____	art	_____	_____	_____
_____	_____	_____	_____	_____
_____	_____	_____	_____	_____
_____	_____	_____	_____	_____

Unit 2 was

interesting ☐   quite interesting ☐   not very interesting ☐

3 What have you got?

1 Key vocabulary *Everyday things*

There's a problem with the computer. The letters *a, e, i, o, u* are missing. Write the correct words.

1	clcltr	6	ky
2	mbrll	7	tnns rckt
3	crsps	8	wtch
4	tsss	9	nrk
5	pncl cs	10	bdg

1 <u>calculator</u> 6 _____

2 _____ 7 _____

3 _____ 8 _____

4 _____ 9 _____

5 _____ 10 _____

2 *a, an* or *some*? G ➤ 15a, 15b

Complete the sentences. Use *a, an* or *some*.

1 I live in Plymouth. Plymouth is <u>a</u>  city in the southwest of England.

2 I've got _____ sister and _____ brother and _____ pets.

3 Today I've got _____ umbrella, _____ crisps and _____ apple in my bag.

4 I've got _____ photos of Cristiano Ronaldo.

5 Cristiano is _____ footballer. He's in *Hello!* this week.

6 *Hello!* is _____ English magazine.

Cristiano Ronaldo

3 *some* or *any*? G ➤ 19a, 19b

Complete the sentences. Use *some* or *any*.

1 Have you got __<u>any</u>__ football socks?

2 I've got _____ socks, but I haven't got _____ football socks.

3 Have you got _____ brothers or sisters?

4 I haven't got _____ sisters.

5 Have you got _____ American friends?

6 I've got _____ English friends, but I haven't got _____ American friends.

7 Have you got _____ photos of England?

8 Yes, I've got _____ photos of London.

4 *have got*: affirmative and negative G ➤ 10a, 10b

Complete the sentences. Use the right form of *have got* and *haven't got*.

Joe   **Sadie and Lisa**   **Barney and Lee**

1 JOE: I've got a three and two fours, but I haven't _____ a six.

2 SADIE: Lisa and I _____ _____ a five, a two and a four, but we _____ _____ a six.

3 JOE: Barney and Lee _____ got a one, a five and a three, but _____ _____ _____ a six.

5 have got: questions and short answers (G) 10c, 10d

Put the words in the right order and make questions. Then write true answers.

1 badges / you / have / got / any ?

Have you got any badges?
Yes, I have.
or _No, I haven't._

2 have / calculator / got / a / you ?

....

....

....

3 Sadie / Lisa / and / tissues / have / any / got ?

....

....

....

4 a / and / Joe / Sadie / have / tortoise / got ?

....

....

....

5 they / snake / a / have / got ?

....

....

....

6 you / dictionary / a / got / have ?

....

....

....

6 Reading *A friend in Canada*

Read the information about Ross. Then complete his email.

Name: **Ross Kennedy**
Nationality: **Canadian**
Age: **13**
Family: **1 sister**
Pets: **1 cat, 2 dogs**
Favourite music: **hip-hop**
Interests: **Skateboarding, computer games**

⬆Previous ⬇Next | Reply Reply all | Print | 🗑

From: ross.kennedy@goline.ca
To: newfriends@lineplus.com
Subject: Write to me!

Hi! My name 's Ross Kennedy. I'............. Canadian and I'...............
thirteen years old. I'............. .... sister, but I ....
got .... brothers. We'............. .... cat and
.... dogs. What about you? Have you .... pets? My
favourite music .... hip-hop and I like skateboarding and computer
games. Have .... skateboard? .... you
.... computer games?

Write soon!

Ross

7 Extension *Reply to Ross*

Write a reply to Ross. Use words from his email.

⬆Previous ⬇Next | Reply Reply all | Print | 🗑

From: ....
To: ross.kennedy@goline.ca
Subject: Re: Write to me!

....

....

....

....

....

....

Write soon!

....

1 Possessive ′s G→ 20a

Complete the sentences. Use the possessive ′s.

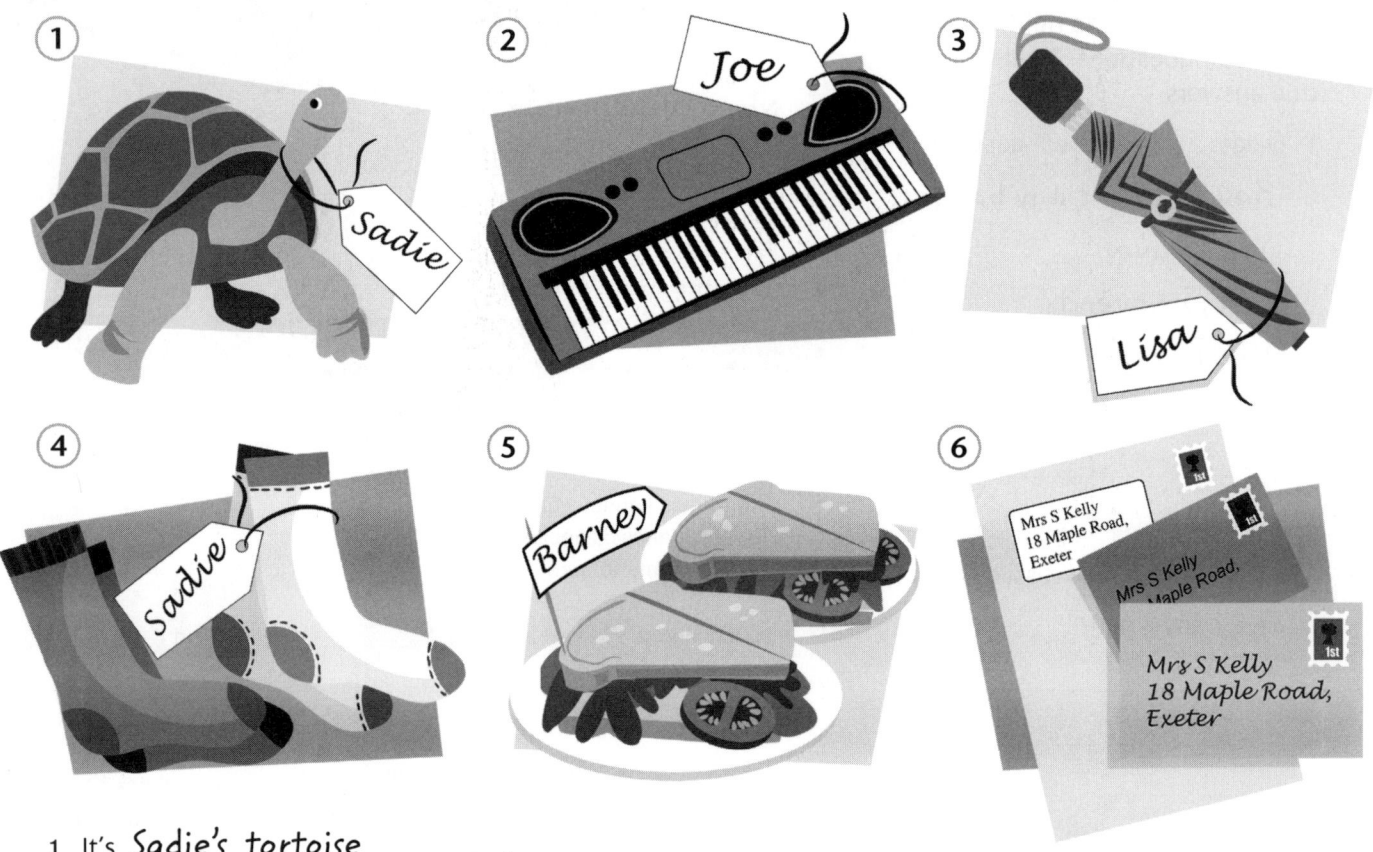

1 It's <u>Sadie's tortoise</u> .

2 It's _____ .

3 It's _____ .

4 They're _____ .

5 They're _____ .

6 They're _____ .

2 ′s: is or possessive ′s? G→ 20a

Look at the words with ′s. Put them in the right list.

	′s = is	′s = possessive
1 She's Joe's sister.	She's	Joe's
2 He's Sadie's brother.		
3 Kate's Sadie and Joe's sister.		
4 It's Sadie's tortoise.		
5 Lisa's Sadie's best friend.		
6 What's the dog's name?		

3 Possessive adjectives

G→ 21a, 21b, 21c

Complete Sadie's answers.
Use *my*, *his*, *her*, *our* or *their*.

1 What's your name?

_____My_____ name's Sadie.

2 What's your brother's name?

_____ name's Joe.

3 What's your sister's name?

_____ name's Kate.

4 What about your parents?

_____ names are Mike

and Sue.

5 Who's Sam?

He's _____ dog!

6 What's your best friend's name?

_____ name's Lisa.

4 What's the reply?

Look at the questions. Circle the right answer: a, b or c.

1 What's your sister's name?
   a My name's Helen.
   b Her name's Helen.
   c His name's Helen.

2 Where's your mobile?
   a It's my mobile.
   b Yes, it is.
   c It's in my pocket.

3 Are you David's cousin?
   a No. I'm his sister.
   b No. I'm her brother.
   c No. I'm her sister.

4 Have you got Joe and Sadie's number?
   a Yes. Their number's 802465.
   b Yes. Our number's 802465.
   c Yes. I know his number.

5 this/that, these/those (G) 16a

What is the woman saying? Complete her sentences.
Use *Is* or *Are* + *this*, *that*, *these* or *those*.

1 **Is this**   your mobile?

2 _____ _____ your apple?

3 _____ _____ your football socks?

4 _____ _____ your sandwiches?

6 Extension

Dad's favourite singer

Complete the conversation.
Write the letters a–h.

a	Have you got Sadie's CD?
b	No, I haven't.
~~c~~	~~Yes?~~
d	I don't know.
e	Yes, I have.
f	Who's that?
g	It isn't in my room.
h	No, it isn't.

SADIE: Joe!

JOE: ¹ *c*

SADIE: Have you got my Joss Stone CD?

JOE: ² _____ I don't like her songs.

SADIE: Where is it?

JOE: ³ _____ Look in your room.

SADIE: ⁴ _____

JOE: Is it in your CD player?

SADIE: ⁵ _____

JOE: Listen! ⁶ _____

SADIE: It's Joss Stone! In the kitchen!

JOE: Dad! ⁷ _____

MR KELLY: ⁸ _____ It's good. I like Joss Stone.

1 Key vocabulary *Families*

a Complete the table.

grandmother	¹*grandfather*
2 _____	father
wife	3 _____
4 _____	son
5 _____	brother
aunt	6 _____
cousin	cousin
parents and ⁷ _____	

b Complete the sentences.

1 My mother's sister is my

_____ .

2 My father's brother is my

_____ .

3 My mother and father are my

_____ .

4 My sister and I are my mother

and father's _____ .

5 My mother's mother is my

_____ .

6 My father's father is my

_____ .

7 My aunt's son or daughter is

my _____ .

8 Joe is Mr Kelly's

_____ .

9 Sadie is Mr Kelly's

_____ .

10 Mrs Kelly is Mr Kelly's

_____ .

2 Listening *Family photos*

Listen to five people talking about their family photos. Find the right photo for each person. Write *1–5* in the boxes.

A

B 1

C

D

E

3 Extension *Members of the family*

Read Mel's sentence. Then write true sentences for the other members of her family.

MEL: I've got a father, a mother, two sisters and a brother.

MEL'S FATHER: I've got *a wife and four* _____ .

MEL'S MOTHER: I've got _____

_____ .

MEL'S BROTHER: I've got _____

_____ .

MEL'S SISTER, LAUREN: I've got _____

_____ .

Unit 3 Learning diary

Date _____

At the end of Unit 3 I can:

	Easy	Not bad	Difficult

- talk about my possessions using *have got*. ☐ ☐ ☐

  I've _____ .

- use *a*, *an*, *some* and *any*. ☐ ☐ ☐

  I've got _____ calculator, _____ umbrella and _____ crisps.

  I haven't got _____ peanuts.   Have you got _____ tissues?

- use *'s* to say that something belongs to someone. ☐ ☐ ☐

  Joe's mobile = _____ *(in my language)*

- remember possessive adjectives. ☐ ☐ ☐

  my, your, _____

- use possessive adjectives. ☐ ☐ ☐

  This is Jack and this is his bike.   = _____

  This is Sadie and this is her brother.   = _____

KEY WORDS

Everyday things		Family	
badge	_____	daughter	_____
_____	_____	_____	_____
_____	_____	_____	_____
_____	_____	_____	_____
_____	_____	_____	_____
_____	_____	_____	_____

Unit 3 was

interesting ☐   quite interesting ☐   not very interesting ☐

4 Descriptions

1 Key vocabulary *Adjectives*

Look at the adjectives in the box. Write a pair of opposites for each picture.

> big   sad   old   small   difficult   good   exciting   noisy   ~~funny~~
> happy   boring   quiet   ~~serious~~   new   easy   bad

funny   serious

....

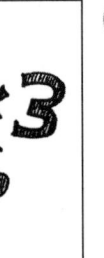 

....

....

....

....

....

2 What's it like?

Complete the conversations. Use *What's he/she/it like?* or *What are they like?*.

1 A: I've got a new anorak.

   B: What's it like? ....

   A: It's blue and white.

2 A: We've got two new students in our class.

   B: ....

   A: They're very nice.

3 A: My sister has got a new boyfriend.

   B: ....

   A: He's very quiet.

4 A: I've got a computer game called *Help!*.

   B: ....

   A: It's quite difficult.

5 A: I've got five brothers.

   B: ....

   A: They're noisy.

6 A: Our new English teacher is called Mrs Green.

   B: ....

   A: She's great.

3 Position of adjectives G→ 22c

Put the words in the right order and make sentences.

1 Will / Smith / an / film / star / American / is

   Will Smith is an American film star.

2 is / sport / a / dangerous / sky surfing

   ....

3 pop / star / your / who's / favourite ?

   ....

4 an / he's / dancer / awful

   ....

5 noisy / I / city / in / live / a

   ....

6 got / serious / I've / problem / a

   ....

4 Reading *Favourite things*

a Look at the pictures and find Tanya's favourite things. Write the correct letters.

TANYA: I like big cities and noisy music. I like the cinema and my favourite films are funny films. I'm Interested In dangerous sports, and I like really difficult computer games. Books aren't my favourite things!

Pictures *F* , ... , ... , ... and ....

b The other five pictures are Luke's favourite things. Complete his list. Use the nouns and adjectives in the box.

quiet	TV programmes	~~easy~~	music	old
serious	films	sad	~~computer games~~	cars

LUKE: My favourite things are *easy computer games,*

....

....

....

5 Extension *Definitions*

These sentences are wrong! Put the descriptions in the right place and make correct sentences.

1 New York is a funny TV programme.

   No! New York is ....

2 *The Lord of the Rings* is a small car.

   No! *The Lord of the Rings* is ....

3 Sky surfing is an American city.

   No! Sky surfing is ....

4 Liverpool is a famous book and a film.

   No! Liverpool is ....

5 A Ford Ka is an English city.

   No! A Ford Ka is ....

6 *The Simpsons* is an exciting sport.

   No! *The Simpsons* is ....

1 Key vocabulary *Appearance and personality*

a Look at the four boys, Harry, Tom, Pete and Sam. Read the sentences. Who's who? Write their names.

Sam has got long, dark, straight hair, and he's got a T-shirt. Pete has got a white T-shirt and short, dark, curly hair. Harry has got fair hair and glasses. He hasn't got a very friendly face. Tom has got curly hair. He hasn't got glasses and he isn't very tall.

A is _____ . B is _____ .

C is _____ . D is _____ .

b Complete the sentences about the boys. <u>Underline</u> the right adjective.

1 I like Sam. He's very (*cruel* / *friendly*).

2 Pete's very (*boring* / *nice*). He's got a lot of friends.

3 Harry has got a lot of homework today. He isn't very (*happy* / *honest*).

4 Tom isn't cruel. He's very (*dangerous* / *kind*).

2 *has got* or *have got*?

 10a

Write these sentences in a different way. Use the right form of *have got*.

1 His hair is long.

   He's got long hair.

2 Her nose is long.

   She _____ *a long nose.*

3 Our eyes are blue.

   We _____

4 My legs are short.

   _____

5 Their T-shirts are white.

   _____

6 Your face is red.

   _____

3 *hasn't got* or *haven't got*? G 10b

What's the problem? Write sentences with *hasn't got* or *haven't got*. Use the words in the box.

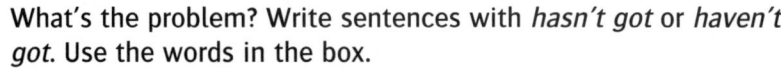

umbrella   surfboard   map   ~~key~~

1 *She hasn't got a key.*

2 *They* _____

3 _____

4 _____

4 has/have got: questions and short answers G→ 10c. 10d

Look at the information in the table. Write questions for answers 1–4, and answers for questions 5–8.

	brown eyes	blue eyes	fair hair	dark hair
Tina	✓	✗	✗	✓
Tanya	✓	✗	✓	✗
Tom	✗	✓	✓	✗

1 *Has Tanya got* .... fair hair?

   Yes, she has.

2 .... fair hair?

   No, she hasn't.

3 .... dark hair?

   No, he hasn't.

4 ....

   brown eyes?

   Yes, they have.

5 Has Tom got blue eyes?

   ....

6 Has Tina got brown eyes?

   ....

7 Have Tanya and Tom got dark hair?

   ....

8 Has Tanya got blue eyes?

   ....

5 Listening *A new friend*

🎧 Listen to Sadie and Pete talking about Pete's family. Circle the right sentence: a, b or c.

1 a Pete has got a brother.
  b Pete hasn't got any sisters.
  c Pete has got a sister.

2 a Helen is thirty.
  b Helen is thirteen.
  c Helen is Sadie's sister.

3 a Helen hasn't got dark hair.
  b Helen has got short, fair hair.
  c Helen's very tall.

4 a Pete and his sister haven't got any pets.
  b Pete's sister has got a cat called Sidney.
  c Pete and his sister have got a snake and a cat.

6 Extension *A pet for sale*

a Read the *For sale* notice. Choose the correct picture. Write A, B or C on the notice.

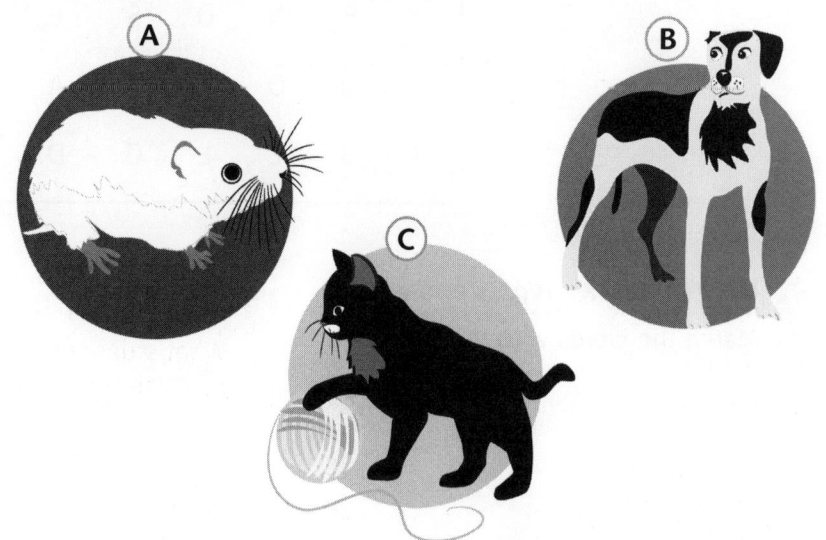

FOR SALE
'Basil'
• 8 months
• Only 1 ear
• Black & white
• V. friendly
£18

Picture ....

b Tick (✓) the correct sentences.

1 It's eighteen months old.   ....

2 It's very friendly.   ....

3 It hasn't got any ears.   ....

4 It's got a name.   ....

5 It's only got one eye.   ....

6 It hasn't got a price.   ....

1 Key vocabulary
Parts of the body

Find ten parts of the body in the word square. Write the words.

1 .... *heart* ....
2 ....
3 ....
4 ....
5 ....
6 ....
7 ....
8 ....
9 ....
10 ....

H	E	A	R	T	P	F
A	Y	R	I	A	O	A
N	E	M	O	R	T	C
D	M	O	U	T	H	E
Y	B	N	O	S	E	T
F	O	O	T	T	A	O
A	B	L	E	G	D	M

2 Word work *Words in the song*
Match the words with the pictures.

| heavy | empty | aeroplane | ~~sad~~ | heart | fed up |

1 ...... *sad* ......   2 ....   3 ....

4 ....   5 ....   6 ....

3 Key vocabulary
How are you?

Make sentences.

1 I / cold
I've got a cold.
....

2 She / stomach ache
....
....

3 We / fine
....
....

4 You / tired
....
....

5 They / fed up
....
....

6 Joe / headache
....
....

4 Extension *Odd one out*
Which word is the odd one out?

1 dangerous (mouth) difficult easy

2 eye heart long leg

3 surfboard happiness tennis racket mountain bike

4 black empty red blue

5 serious honest tall friendly

6 tonight today teacher this morning

7 octopus apple hamster dog

8 curly quiet dark fair

Unit 4 Learning diary

Date _____

At the end of Unit 4 I can:

	Easy	Not bad	Difficult
describe things and places.	☐	☐	☐

Computer games are _____ . Our town is _____ .

It's a very exciting film = _____ *(in my language)*

	Easy	Not bad	Difficult
talk about appearance and personality.	☐	☐	☐

I've got _____ eyes and _____ hair. I _____ glasses.
I'm _____ .
Mr Hyde has got _____ . He's a _____ person.

	Easy	Not bad	Difficult
ask for a description.	☐	☐	☐

What's your new game like? = _____ *(in my language)*

What are Joe and Sadie like? = _____

	Easy	Not bad	Difficult
talk about how I feel.	☐	☐	☐

I'm fed up. = _____ *(in my language)*

I've got a cold. = _____

I've got a headache. = _____

KEY WORDS

Adjectives		Appearance and personality		Parts of the body
exciting	_____	fair	honest	hand
_____	_____	_____	_____	_____
_____	_____	_____	_____	_____
_____	_____	_____	_____	_____
_____	_____	_____	_____	_____

Unit 4 was

interesting ☐   quite interesting ☐   not very interesting ☐

1 Key vocabulary *Things you do*

Look at the verbs in the circles.
Cross out the words that don't fit.

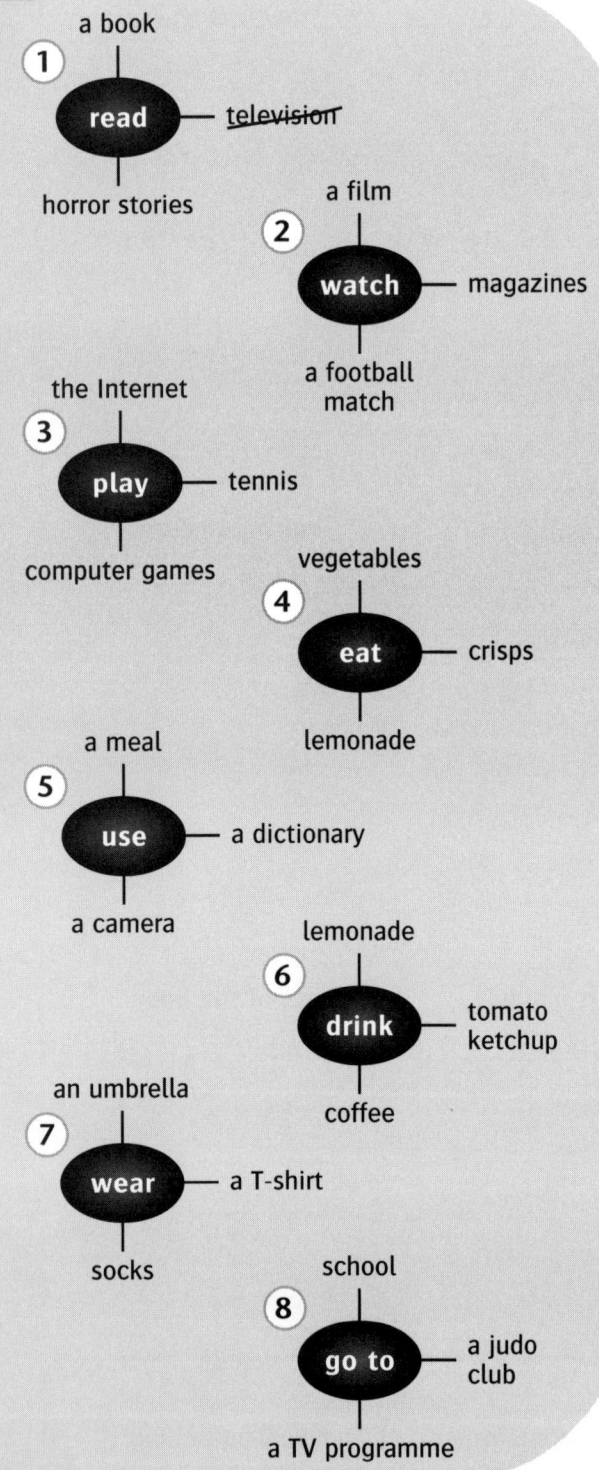

1. read — a book — ~~television~~ — horror stories
2. watch — a film — magazines — a football match
3. play — the Internet — tennis — computer games
4. eat — vegetables — crisps — a meal — lemonade
5. use — a dictionary — a camera
6. drink — lemonade — tomato ketchup — coffee
7. wear — an umbrella — a T-shirt — socks
8. go to — school — a judo club — a TV programme

2 Present simple: *I live ...* G→ 5a. 5d

Complete Luke's letter to his Spanish pen friend. Use the verbs in the box.

eat	like	go (x2)	~~live~~	read	watch	listen
write	use					

Dear César,

My name's Luke Harris. I ¹ __live__ in London and I ² _____ to Marsden College in Camden. I'm a basketball addict! I ³ _____ to a basketball club every Friday and I ⁴ _____ a lot of magazines about basketball. After school I ⁵ _____ TV or I ⁶ _____ to music. I ⁷ _____ rap.

I've got a computer. I ⁸ _____ emails to my friends and I ⁹ _____ the Internet. My favourite food is hamburger and chips, and I ¹⁰ _____ a lot of pizzas too.

Write soon!

Luke

3 Present simple: *He lives ...* G→ 5a. 5e

Write ten sentences about Luke Harris.

1. He lives in London.
2. He _____ to Marsden College.
3. He _____
4. _____
5. _____
6. _____
7. _____
8. _____
9. _____
10. _____

4 Present simple: *live or lives?* (G) ➤ 5a

Underline the right verb form.

Hi! My name's Roxanne. I'm Lee Harper's sister. We ¹ (*live* / *lives*) in Exeter, but our parents ² (*come* / *comes*) from Jamaica. We ³ (*like* / *likes*) music in our house. My brother Lee ⁴ (*like* / *likes*) rap. My father ⁵ (*love* / *loves*) reggae, but my mother ⁶ (*prefer* / *prefers*) rock music. I ⁷ (*play* / *plays*) the piano and I ⁸ (*prefer* / *prefers*) Mozart!

5 Spelling: *s or es?* (G) ➤ 5e

Complete the sentences. Write the correct form of the verbs. Look at the spelling notes on page 142 in the Student's Book.

1 Mark ____lives____ in Australia. (*live*)
2 My tortoise _____ vegetables. (*eat*)
3 My sister _____ to a judo club. (*go*)
4 My friend Adil _____ from Morocco. (*come*)
5 He _____ every football match on TV. (*watch*)
6 Sadie _____ the Internet every day. (*use*)

6 Present simple: affirmative and negative (G) ➤ 5b

Look at the information in the table. Are the sentences true or false? Correct the false sentences.

	Musical instrument	Computer	French	Sport	Horror films
Sadie	Yes	Yes	Yes	No	No
Jack	No	Yes	Yes	No	Yes

1 Jack plays a musical instrument.

   False. Jack doesn't play a musical instrument.

2 Sadie uses a computer.

   True.

3 Sadie and Jack don't learn French at school.

   ----

4 Jack watches sport on TV.

   ----

5 Sadie likes horror films.

   ----

6 Sadie doesn't watch sport on TV.

   ----

7 Sadie and Jack watch sport on TV.

   ----

8 Sadie doesn't play a musical instrument.

   ----

7 Extension *Your favourite days*

Write sentences about a day you like and a day you don't like.

I like Tuesday because I go to the swimming club after school. I don't like Monday because ...

----

1 Present simple: questions and short answers (G) → 5c, 5f

Match the questions with the answers.

1 Do Joe and Sadie live in London?
2 Do they go to Westover School?
3 Does Joe play in a band?
4 Does he play hockey?
5 Does Sadie read horror stories?
6 Do you live in London?
7 Do you go to school?

a Yes, he does.
b Yes, I do.
c No, I don't.
d No, she doesn't.
e No, he doesn't.
f No, they don't.
g Yes, they do.

1 _f_   2 ____   3 ____   4 ____   5 ____   6 ____   7 ____

2 Question forms

What animals is Martin scared of? Complete the questions with *Do, Does, Have* or *Are* and read the answers. Then guess the name of the animals.

1 A: _____Do_____ they live in the sea?

B: No, they don't.

2 A: _____ they live near houses?

B: Yes, they do.

3 A: _____ Martin see them in the bathroom?

B: No, he doesn't.

4 A: _____ they got eight legs?

B: No, they haven't.

5 A: _____ they eat our food?

B: Yes, they do.

6 A: _____ the letters *ats* in their name?

B: Yes, they are.

7 A: _____ they bats?

B: No, they aren't.

Martin is scared

of _____ .

3 Find the questions (G) → 5c, 5f

a Put the words in the right order and make questions. In each group, circle the word you don't use.

1 eat / do /(Sadie)/ you / meat ?

Do you eat meat?

2 use / like / does / Joe / vegetables ?

_____

_____

3 Joe / football / Internet / play / and / basketball / does ?

_____

_____

4 do / does / Joe / Sadie / and / music / like ?

_____

_____

5 do / speak / the / you / French ?

_____

_____

b Now make a question with the words in the circles.

6 _____

_____

c Answer questions 1–6.

1 _Yes, I do._ or _No, I don't._

2 _____

3 _____

4 _____

5 _____

6 _____

4 Key vocabulary *Scary things*

Find a word for each picture and write the complete poem. Write a title for the poem.

There's a [spider] on my head,

And an [monster] is in my bed.

There's [thunder] Booooom! in the dark.

In the bathroom there's a [shark] .

A [ghost] is on the stairs,

And scary [mice] in pairs.

In the garden ten black cats,

A [UFO] and two [bats] .

Title: ....

....

....

....

....

....

....

5 Reading *What is it?*

Read the descriptions. What's the word for each description?

1 It's got three hundred and sixty-five days.   y e a r

2 These aren't magazines, but they've got pictures and words.

Children read them.   c ....

3 Are you scared when you see this at the cinema?

h ....   f ....

4 We make windows with this.   g ....

5 They visit other countries when they go on holiday.

t ....

6 Listening *What do they like?*

[cassette] Listen to three teenagers. What are their interests?
Put a tick (✓) for the things they like and a cross (✗) for
the things they don't like.

		Television	Sport	Computers	Books	Music
1	Tom					✓
2	Anna					
3	Rick					

7 Extension *Make sentences*

Write at least five true sentences
about Tom, Anna and Rick.

Tom likes music.

....

....

....

....

....

....

....

....

....

1 Wh- questions ⓖ→ 14

Complete the questions.
Use *What, What sort of,
Who, Where, When* or *Why*.

1 A: ......*What*......

   subjects does Joe like

   at school?

   B: Maths and history.

2 A: ....

   language does Sadie

   learn at school?

   B: French.

3 A: ....

   music does Joe like?

   B: Rap and hip-hop.

4 A: ....

   doesn't eat meat?

   B: Sadie.

5 A: .... does

   Sadie play hockey?

   B: At school.

6 A: .... does

   Sadie go to the judo

   club?

   B: On Friday.

7 A: .... do

   Joe and Sadie want

   to go to Australia?

   B: Because they want

   to see their cousins.

2 Dialogue completion

A conversation with Tiger Woods

Tiger Woods is a famous American golfer. Complete the conversation with the questions. Write the letters a–g.

a What are your interests?
b Why do you wear a red T-shirt when you play?
c What sort of food do you like?
d What sort of computer games do you play?
e̶ ̶W̶h̶e̶r̶e̶ ̶d̶o̶ ̶y̶o̶u̶ ̶l̶i̶v̶e̶?̶
f Who's your favourite sportsperson?
g Why are you called Tiger?

QUESTION: Tiger, [1] *e*

TIGER: In Orlando, Florida.

QUESTION: Your name is Eldrick. [2] ......

TIGER: Because my father likes the name.

QUESTION: [3] ......

TIGER: Cheeseburgers.

QUESTION: [4] ......

TIGER: I like computer games.

QUESTION: [5] ......

TIGER: Golf games.

QUESTION: [6] ......

TIGER: The basketball star, Michael Jordan.

QUESTION: [7] ......

TIGER: Because my mother thinks it's my special colour!

3 Extension *Write about you*

a Answer the questions.

   What sort of music do you like? ....

   Where do you go at the weekend? ....

b Think of other questions and write your answers.

....?

....?

....?

....

Unit 5 Learning diary

Date _____

At the end of Unit 5 I can:

	Easy	Not bad	Difficult
• talk about things I do at home and at school.	☐	☐	☐

I use a computer. I _____ .

| • talk about my friends. | ☐ | ☐ | ☐ |

We say *I play volleyball.* but *He play_____ volleyball.* We use an *s* after _____ .

| • describe my likes and dislikes. | ☐ | ☐ | ☐ |

I like _____ . *I don't like* _____ .

| • ask questions about likes and dislikes. | ☐ | ☐ | ☐ |

Do you like _____ ? _____ *Joe like history?*

| • ask questions about daily life with* What, Where,* etc. | ☐ | ☐ | ☐ |

Where do you _____ ?
What sort of _____ ?

| • talk about scary things. | ☐ | ☐ | ☐ |

I'm scared of _____ .
I don't believe in _____ .

KEY WORDS

Verbs	Likes and dislikes	Scary things
go	*magazines*	*thunder*

Unit 5 was

interesting ☐   quite interesting ☐   not very interesting ☐

6 I'm usually late!

1 Word work *Animals*

Find the names of 12 animals in the wordsquare. Then write the names under the pictures.

```
E D O G I C A T
G O R I L L A O
O L L A B E X R
S P I D E R O T
N H O B A R K O
A I N U R A T I
K N S H A R K S
E G I R A F F E
```

1 ___spider___   2 _____   3 _____

4 _____   5 _____   6 _____

7 _____   8 _____   9 _____

10 _____   11 _____   12 _____

2 Frequency adverbs (G) ➔ 23a

Underline the right words.

1 Lions (*sometimes* / *always*) eat meat.
2 Snakes are (*usually* / *never*) scared of people.
3 Bears (*never* / *sometimes*) attack people.
4 Dolphins are (*always* / *usually*) friendly.
5 Sharks are (*sometimes* / *never*) dangerous.
6 Giraffes (*sometimes* / *never*) eat other animals.
7 You (*often* / *don't often*) find rats in big cities.
8 Spiders (*don't often* / *often*) kill people.

3 Position of frequency adverbs (G) ➔ 23b, 23c

What do you do at the weekend? Add *always*, *usually*, *often*, *sometimes* or *never* and make true sentences.

1 I see my friends.   ___I often see my friends.___
2 I go to the cinema. _____
3 I watch videos.   _____
4 I'm bored.   _____
5 I visit my grandparents. _____
6 I play … (*a sport*) _____
7 I don't tidy my room. _____
8 I'm lazy.   _____

4 Word order G→ 23b, 23c

Put the words in the right order and make sentences.
Then match the sentences with the pictures.

1 is / shop / the / open / always

   *The shop is always open.*_____ Picture *B*

2 tidy / his / often / doesn't / room / he

   _____ Picture _____

3 are / hungry / always / you ?

   _____ Picture _____

4 always / isn't / happy / Emma

   _____ Picture _____

5 he / cleans / never / his / bike

   _____ Picture _____

6 usually / do / on / you / floor / sleep / the ?

   _____ Picture _____

7 for / school / is / late / Louise / sometimes

   _____ Picture _____

5 What are you like?

Match the sentences in A with the sentences in B.

A	B
1 I'm always happy.	a I use the Internet every day.
2 I'm lazy.	b I often do things for other people.
3 I'm a computer addict.	c I don't often tidy my room.
4 I'm very energetic.	d I haven't got any problems.
5 I'm usually helpful.	e I never forget important things.
6 I'm very well-organised.	f I play a lot of sport.

1 *d*   2 _____   3 _____   4 _____   5 _____   6 _____

6 Extension *What is it?*

Write a description of an animal, a person or a thing. Can your teacher guess what it is?

It lives in the sea. It's usually in a group. It sometimes plays with people in the sea. What is it?

Answer: a dolphin.

_____

_____

_____

_____

1 Key vocabulary *Food and drink*

a Read the three descriptions. Write *Sadie*, *Joe* and *Ben* under the right pictures.

> For dinner I usually have pasta with cheese and salad. I like bread and butter with my pasta. Then I have yoghurt with an apple or a banana.

Sadie

> I always have lunch in the school canteen. I often have chicken and chips with vegetables, and I have a can of apple juice. I sometimes have yoghurt too.

Ben

> On Sunday, I usually have a big breakfast. I have cereal, then I have eggs and sausages with toast. And I drink fruit juice or tea.

Joe

A

B

C

D

b The other picture is Mr Kelly's lunch. Complete the description.

Mr Kelly has _____

_____

2 Listening *The school canteen*

🔊 Listen to Mel, Barney and Lee in the school canteen. Circle the right answer: a, b or c.

1 Who wants a fruit salad?
  a Mel.
  b Lee.
  c Barney.

2 Does Lee want a banana yoghurt?
  a Yes, he does.
  b No, he doesn't.
  c He isn't sure.

3 Who doesn't want a drink?
  a Barney.
  b Mel.
  c Lee.

4 What sort of salad does Mel want?
  a A green salad.
  b A fruit salad.
  c A chicken salad.

5 Who wants fruit juice?
  a Barney.
  b Mel.
  c Lee.

6 Who wants meat?
  a Mel and Barney.
  b Barney and Lee.
  c Lee and Mel.

3 *have* Ⓖ➜ 10f

Complete the sentences. Use the right form of the verb *have*.

1 I sometimes __*have*__ breakfast in bed.

2 I never _____ milk in my tea.

3 Ben always _____ toast for breakfast.

4 He never _____ tea or coffee.

5 _____ Lisa sometimes _____ lunch in the canteen?

6 What _____ you usually _____ for lunch?

7 We usually _____ cheese sandwiches.

8 When _____ Joe and Sadie usually _____ dinner?

4 Reading *The snake, the fox and the shark*

Read the text. Are the sentences true or false?

1 The anaconda often eats animals. _True._

2 After a big meal it usually sleeps for a year. ....

3 English foxes don't all live in towns. ....

4 The fox often has dinner in the street. ....

5 The great white shark never attacks other fish. ....

6 It isn't always very dangerous. ....

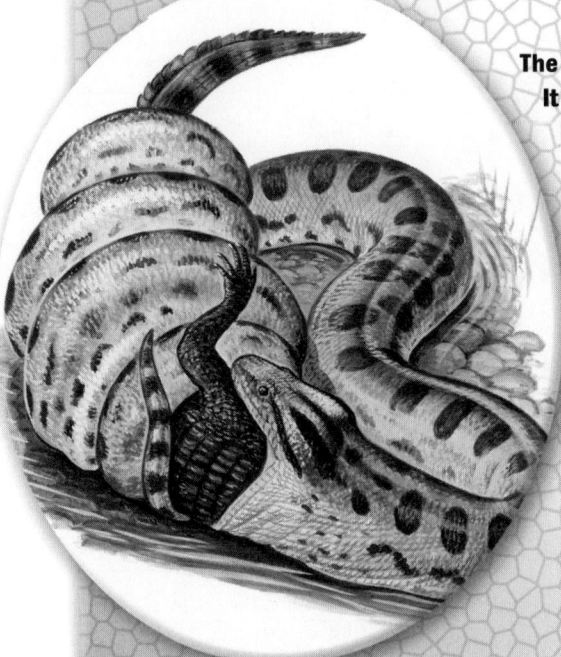

The anaconda is a big snake. It eats fish, animals and birds. It sometimes has a small crocodile for lunch! After a big meal it often sleeps for three or four weeks. Then it doesn't usually eat for at least a year.

The great white shark has got a lot of teeth and it isn't always friendly! It usually eats fish. It doesn't often attack people. But surfers in Australia don't like it because it's sometimes very dangerous.

In England a lot of foxes live in towns now. They often find their food in the street at night. It's in big black bags. They sometimes have sausages and chips, pizza and spaghetti for dinner!

5 What do they have for lunch?

Complete the names of the things in each lunchbox. Use the words in the box. Which lunchbox is Joe's and which is Sadie's? (Look at page 50 in the Student's Book.)

| bananas | sandwich | crisps | packet | can | bottle | apple | chicken |

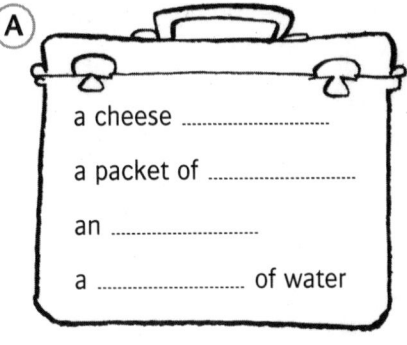

Ⓐ

a cheese ....

a packet of ....

an ....

a .... of water

Ⓑ

a .... sandwich

a .... of peanuts

two ....

a .... of lemonade

A is ....'s lunchbox.

B is ....'s lunchbox.

6 Extension

Your lunchbox

What do you want in your lunchbox? Write a list.

....

....

....

....

....

....

....

....

1 Key vocabulary *The time*

Write the clock times in words.

1 8.10 ten past eight

2 11.05 ....

3 9.15 ....

4 10.40 ....

5 12.00 ....

6 11.55 ....

7 7.30 ....

8 4.45 ....

9 3.35 ....

10 1.25 ....

2 Rick's routine

a Put the pictures in the right order. Write *1–8* in the boxes.

A 8:40am

B 10:30pm

C 8:15am

D 7:15am [1]

E 7:40am

F 7:30pm

G 4:30pm

H 7:20am

b Write a sentence for each picture. Use the words in the box.

go to bed   ~~get up~~
do his homework   catch
get home   get to
have a shower   have breakfast

1 Rick gets up at quarter past seven.

2 He ....

....

3 ....

....

4 ....

....

5 ....

....

6 ....

....

7 ....

....

8 ....

....

c Complete the questions about Rick.

1 What time .... he get up?

2 .... does he get home?

3 .... does he do at half past ten?

3 Extension *More questions*

Write three more questions about Rick's routine.

What time ....

.... ?

When ....

.... ?

What ....

.... ?

Unit 6 Learning diary

Date _____

At the end of Unit 6 I can:

	Easy	Not bad	Difficult
• talk about my habits.	☐	☐	☐

I always _____ .

I often _____ .

	Easy	Not bad	Difficult
• remember words for food, drink and meals.	☐	☐	☐

bread, cheese, _____

juice, tea, _____

breakfast, _____

	Easy	Not bad	Difficult
• describe my meals.	☐	☐	☐

I usually have _____ .

	Easy	Not bad	Difficult
• ask for and tell the time.	☐	☐	☐

_____ the time? 🕐 It's one o'clock.

🕓 _____

🕖 _____

🕡 _____

	Easy	Not bad	Difficult
• describe my daily routines.	☐	☐	☐

I get up at _____ . I _____ .

KEY WORDS

Frequency adverbs	Habits and routines		Food and drink	
sometimes	have a meal	_____	sandwich	_____
_____	leave home	_____	_____	_____
_____	_____	_____	_____	_____
_____	_____	_____	_____	_____
_____	_____	_____	_____	_____

Unit 6 was

interesting ☐   quite interesting ☐   not very interesting ☐

7 At home

1 Key vocabulary *Homes*

Read the clues and write the words.

1 You usually sleep here.
2 You clean your teeth here.
3 Big houses have sometimes got a swimming pool outside in the ....
4 When a house has got two floors, the bedrooms are usually ....
5 You do the cooking here.
6 When you open the door and go into the house, you go into the ....
7 The television is usually here.
8 A room where people eat their meals.
9 There isn't a bath in our bathroom, but there's a ....
10 This is the opposite of number 4.

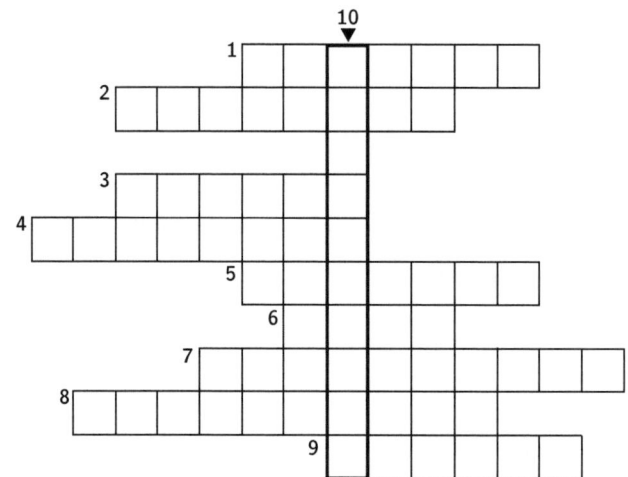

Westover School

Number of students: 980

Number of teachers: ¹ _____

Facilities:

- sports hall
- ² _____ _____
- two gyms
- ³ _____ _____
  _____
- two computer rooms
- ⁴ _____

Activities:

- sports clubs
- music club
- ⁵ _____
  _____

2 Listening

Westover School

a 🔊 Listen to Sadie's interview and complete the details about Westover School.

b Complete the sentences about Westover School. Begin with *There's* or *There are.*

1 *There are nine hundred and eighty* students.

2 *There* _____ _____ _____ - _____ teachers.

3 _____ a sports hall and a _____ _____ .

4 _____ _____ two gyms and four _____ _____ .

5 _____ a _____ room and two _____ _____ .

6 _____ a music club and a _____ _____ .

3 Reading *The Queen's home in London*

Read about Buckingham Palace. Then read the sentences and write *T* (true), *F* (false) or *?* (the answer isn't in the text).

Buckingham Palace is the Queen's home in London. There are six hundred rooms. There's a cinema, a swimming pool and seventy-eight bathrooms.

If you want to know the time, there are three hundred clocks. Outside, there's a very big garden with a lake.

Tourists can visit the palace in August and September. There aren't any ghosts but, if you're bored, go to the White Drawing Room and look at the big mirror. Behind the mirror, there's a secret door!

You can visit the palace now. There's a website with lots of information.

1 Buckingham Palace
  is in London.   .T.

2 There are 68 bathrooms
  in the palace.   ....

3 There isn't a gym.   ....

4 There are a lot of clocks.   ....

5 There isn't a music room.   ....

6 There aren't any tourists
  at the palace in May.   ....

7 There's a big mirror in
  one of the rooms.   ....

8 There's a ghost behind
  the secret door.   ....

4 There is/are G ▶ 11a

Make five sentences from the words in the box.

> two cinemas near here.   ~~There's a~~   pizza in the kitchen.
> There's a   ~~big spider in my hair.~~   there isn't   There aren't
> There are   a key.   any good programmes on TV tonight.

1 Aaagh! *There's a big spider in my hair.*

2 I'm bored. _____

3 Are you hungry? _____

4 The door's locked and _____

5 Do you want to see a film? _____

_____

5 Extension *Your school*

Write at least three true sentences about your school.

There isn't a swimming pool at my school.

_____

_____

_____

_____

1 There is/are + a, an or some 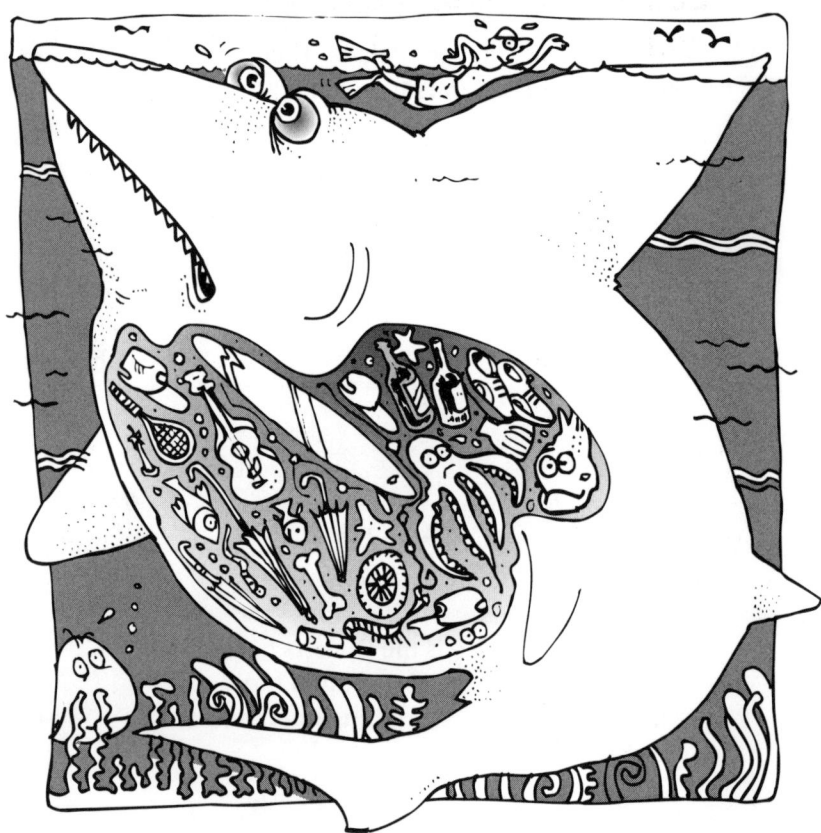 11a, 15a, 15b

What's in the first shark's stomach?
Use *There's* or *There are + a, an* or *some*.

1 *There's a* _____ tennis racket.

2 *There are some* _____ bottles.

3 _____ guitar.

4 _____ umbrellas.

5 _____ surfboard.

6 _____ trainers.

7 _____ octopus.

8 _____ baseball caps.

2 There is/are: questions and short answers 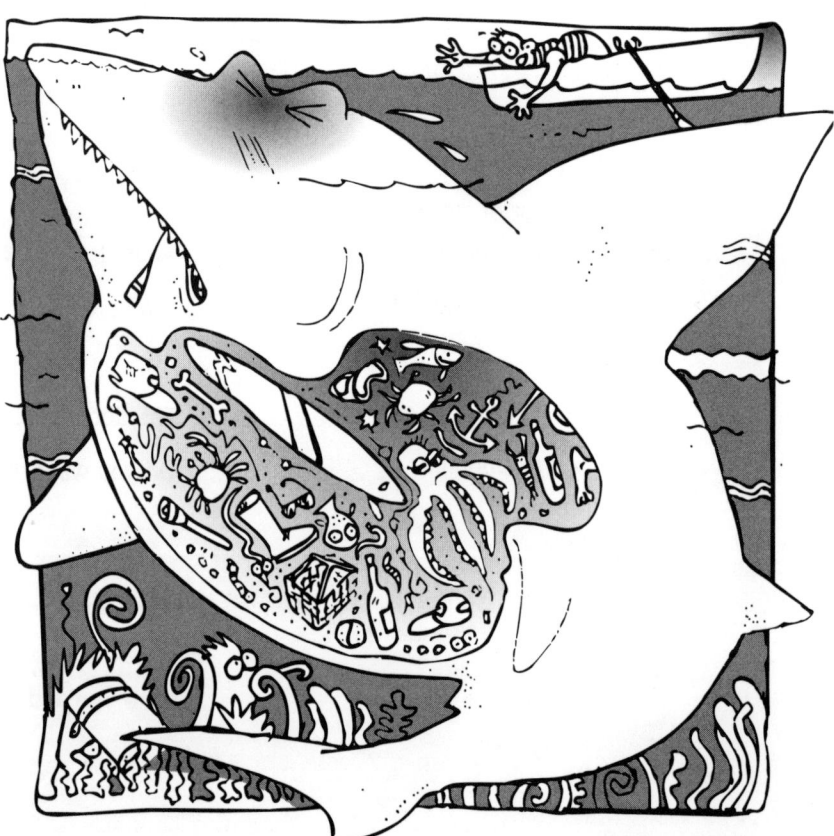 11a, 11c, 19b

What's in the second shark's stomach?
Complete the questions with *Is there / Are there* and *a, an* or *any*. Then write the short answers.

1 *Is there a* _____ tennis racket?
  No, there isn't _____ .

2 *Are there any* _____ bottles?
  _____ , _____ _____ .

3 _____ _____ _____ surfboard?
  _____ , _____ _____ .

4 _____ _____ _____ trainers?
  _____ , _____ _____ .

5 _____ _____ _____ baseball caps?
  _____ , _____ _____ .

6 _____ _____ _____ guitar?
  _____ , _____ _____ .

7 _____ _____ _____ umbrellas?
  _____ , _____ _____ .

8 _____ _____ _____ octopus?
  _____ , _____ _____ .

3 Countable and uncountable nouns (G)→ 18a, 18b, 19b

a Put these things in the cupboard.

milk   can of lemonade   butter
onion   eggs   bottle of water
tomatoes   cheese   bread   apple

b What's in the cupboard?
Write sentences with *There's a/an/some* or *There are some*.

a _can of lemonade_	some _milk_
a _____	some _____
an _____	some _____
an _____	some _____
	some _____
	some _____

1 _There are some tomatoes._

2 _____

3 _____

4 _____

5 _____

6 _____

7 _____

4 There isn't / There aren't + any (G)→ 19a, 19b

Complete the sentences. Use the words in the box.

pasta   fruit juice   paper   bread   eggs   apples

1 I want some orange juice, but there _isn't any fruit juice_ .

2 I want an omelette, but there aren't _____ . _____ .

3 I want a ham sandwich, but _____ _____ _____ .

4 I want some spaghetti, but _____ _____ _____ _____ .

5 I want a fruit salad, but _____ _____ _____ .

6 I want to make a list, but _____ _____ _____ _____ .

5 Extension *At the supermarket*

Choose your favourite food. What is/isn't in your trolley? Write at least four sentences with *There's / There are* or *There isn't / There aren't*.

There's some tomato ketchup.   There aren't any mushrooms.

_____

_____

_____

_____

1 Key vocabulary *Things in a room*

The names of the things are in code. Write the words.

> There's a (*mbnq*) _____ on the (*ubcmf*) _____ .

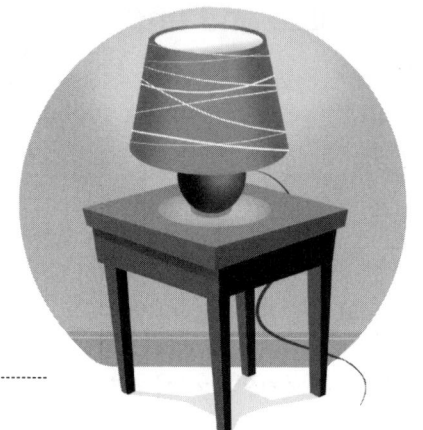

1 eftl _____

2 njssps _____

3 tifmwft _____

4 xbsespcf _____

5 svh _____

6 dmpdl _____

7 dibjs _____

8 diftu pg esbxfst _____

2 Prepositions G➤ 24a

Describe the pictures. Say where the people and animals are. Use the prepositions in the box.

| on | next to | opposite | in front of | ~~under~~ | above | behind | in |

1 *There's a cat under the table.*

2 *There's _____ _____ wall.*

3 _____

4 _____

5 _____
_____

6 _____
_____

7 _____
_____

8 _____
_____

3 Extension *A poem*

Write a poem of six lines. Use prepositions (*under, on, above*, etc.).

There are some ghosts downstairs in the hall.
There's an octopus on the wall.

_____ the hall.

_____ the wall.

_____ the floor.

_____ the door.

_____ my bed.

_____ my head.

Unit 7 Learning diary

Date _____

At the end of Unit 7 I can:

	Easy	Not bad	Difficult
• describe my home and my classroom.	☐	☐	☐

There's a living room _____ .

There are some _____ .

• use countable and uncountable nouns.　　☐　☐　☐

Countable	**Uncountable**
apple _____	*paper* _____
_____	_____
_____	_____

• ask questions about food and drink.　　☐　☐　☐

Is there any _____ ?　　*Are there any* _____ ?

• say where things and people are, using prepositions.

I usually sit next to _____ .

My bag is _____ .

• describe my room.　　☐　☐　☐

There's a _____ .

There are some _____ .

KEY WORDS

Homes	Things in a room	Prepositions
dining room _____	*chest of drawers* _____ _____	*in front of* _____
downstairs _____	_____ _____	_____
_____ _____	_____ _____	_____
_____ _____	_____ _____	_____
_____ _____	_____ _____	_____
_____ _____	_____ _____	_____

Unit 7 was

interesting ☐　　quite interesting ☐　　not very interesting ☐

8 Having fun

1 Key vocabulary *Abilities* G→ 12a, 12b, 12d

Write sentences with *can* or *can't*.

1 *He can stand on his head.*

2 *He* _____

3 *She* _____

4 _____

5 _____

6 _____

 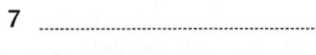

7 _____

8 _____

9 _____

2 *can/can't*: questions and short answers G→ 12c, 12e

Put the words in the right order and make questions. Then write true answers.

1 swim / dogs / can ?

Can dogs swim?

Yes, they can.

2 you / can / Arabic / speak ?

_____

_____

3 the / Joe / play / can / keyboard ?

_____

_____

4 Mel / Adams / sing / can ?

_____

_____

5 horse / you / a / can / ride ?

_____

_____

6 fly / horses / can ?

_____

_____

3 Reading *What can they do?*

Read the text. Then write the age under each picture.

When babies are six weeks old, they can't stand, they can't walk and they can't talk. They can see their mother's face, but they can't see different colours.

At the age of two, children can usually walk and talk and they can stand on one foot. When they are three years old, they can draw lines and circles, but they can't usually read or write. At the age of four, they can often write their name.

At the age of five, they can usually say about 2,000 words. They can say their address and their telephone number. They can often use a computer. When they are six years old, they can ride a bike, and they can usually read. But of course all children are different!

1 Six years old.   2 _____   3 _____

4 _____   5 _____   6 _____

4 What am I?

Can you find the answer to the puzzle?

I'm not a person. I'm a thing.
I can't dance and I can't sing.
I can fly, but I can't walk.
I can be noisy, but I can't talk.
I can go across the world in a day.
What am I? Can you say?

I'm _____ .

5 Extension *Two different children*

Read about Helen and James. Then give the correct information.

Helen is five years old. She can read and write, but she can't play the piano. She can ride a bike, but she can't ride a horse. She can't play tennis, but she can swim two hundred metres in the swimming pool.

James is four years old. He can't write, but he can read and he can play Bach and Mozart on the piano. He can't ride a bike and he can't play football or tennis, but he can swim. He can ride a horse too.

1 Two things they both can do:

They **can read.** _____ . They _____ .

2 One thing they both can't do:

They _____ .

3 Two things Helen can do, but James can't do:

She _____ . She _____ .

4 Two things James can do, but Helen can't do:

He _____ . He _____ .

1 Key vocabulary *Places in a town*

The sentences describe places in a town. Complete the words.

1 You can go here on Sunday and sing. c h u r c h

2 You can go to a lot of different shops here. s _ _ _ _ _ _   c _ _ _ _ _

3 You can catch a train here. s _ _ _ _ _

4 You can have a drink here and write an email. I _ _ _ _ _ _ _   c _ _ _

5 You can catch a bus here. b _ _   s _ _ _ _ _ _

6 You can learn about the history of a town here. m _ _ _ _ _

7 You can see a film here. c _ _ _ _ _

8 You can go for a walk with your dog here. p _ _ _

9 You can watch fish here. a _ _ _ _ _ _ _

10 You can swim and play basketball here. s _ _ _ _ _   c _ _ _ _ _

2 *can't* for impossibility G ➤ 12f

Tom and Gary are bored. Complete the sentences.

1 They can't_____ go bowling,

because there isn't a bowling alley.

2 _____ go _____,

because there isn't a swimming pool.

3 _____ go _____,

because there aren't any shops.

4 _____ see _____,

because there isn't a cinema.

5 _____ go _____

a walk, because it's dark outside.

6 _____ surf _____

_____, because they haven't got

a computer.

3 *can* or *can't*?

Write sentences with *can* or *can't* for these signs.

1 You can get information here.

2 You _____ _____ _____

_____ here.

3 _____ _____ _____ basketball here.

4 _____ _____ _____ _____

_____ here.

5 _____ _____ _____ here.

6 _____ _____ _____ here.

7 _____ _____ _____ _____

_____ _____ here.

8 _____ _____ _____ here.

4 Listening

Where are they?

🔊 Listen and say where the people are. Write the correct letter (a–h) next to each person.

a   a museum
b   a bus station
c   a park
d   an aquarium
e   a shopping centre
f   a cathedral
g   a cinema
h   a station

1   Sue   ......
2   Andy   ......
3   Louise   ......
4   Dan   ......
5   Martha   ......

5 can/can't + see (G) ➔ 12g

Look at the picture puzzle and the words in 1–7. Write sentences with *I can see* or *I can't see*. Use *some* or *any* with the plural nouns.

1   sharks   *I can't see any sharks.*
2   a man's face ....
3   a train   ....
4   cars   ....
5   a plane   ....
6   a horse   ....
7   birds   ....

6 can + see/hear (G) ➔ 12g

Complete the sentences. Use *can/can't see* or *can/can't hear*.

1   Look! You ..... *can see* ..... the moon above the trees.

2   Listen! .... you .... that music?

3   I .... the television. I haven't got my glasses.

4   .... you .... my anorak? I can't find it.

5   Be quiet! I .... my CD.

6   Where are you? I .... you, but I .... you!

7 Extension   *Your dream place*

Imagine you're in your dream place. What sort of things can you do there? What can you see/hear? Write at least four sentences.

I'm in Hawaii. I can see the blue sea.

....

....

....

....

1 must/mustn't (G) 13d

Write the sentences in a different way. Use *must* or *mustn't*.

1 Go to bed!   *You must go to bed.*

2 Don't interrupt me!

3 Don't be silly!

4 Be polite!

5 Wash your hands!

6 Be quiet!

7 Don't listen to him!

8 Don't be late!

9 Tidy your room!

10 Don't say that!

2 Imperative (G) 9a, 9b

What do you say in these situations? Match them with the sentences in the box.

Don't be silly!	Be quiet!
Don't sit down!	~~Look!~~
Don't eat that!	Listen!

1 You're with your friends. You can see a UFO in the sky.

   Look!

2 Your friend wants to walk across the road with his eyes closed.

3 You want to watch something on television. Your brother is talking.

4 Your baby sister has got a key in her mouth.

5 You're at home with a friend. You can hear something outside.

6 There's a spider on your friend's chair. Your friend doesn't know it's there.

3 What's the reply?

Complete the five conversations. Circle the right reply: a, b or c.

1 It's *Top of the Pops* on TV.
   a Oh, yes. We must wash it.
   b I must do my homework.
   c You can't wear that.

2 Can I go to the cinema tonight?
   a What's the problem?
   b No, I can't.
   c It depends.

3 Thanks for a fantastic meal.
   a What do you fancy?
   b You mustn't be rude!
   c You're welcome.

4 Can you tidy your room?
   a Yes, you can. Thanks.
   b Yes, OK.
   c Yes, I know.

5 Can I use your mobile?
   a No, I can't.
   b Sure. Here you are.
   c Is it your mobile?

4 Extension *Give your orders!*

Imagine you're a parent. What do you say to your children? Use the imperative or *must/mustn't*. Write at least four sentences.

You must eat your vegetables. Don't interrupt me!

Unit 8 Learning diary

Date _____

At the end of Unit 8 I can:

	Easy	Not bad	Difficult
• talk about my abilities.	☐	☐	☐

I can _____ but I can't _____ .

| • describe what you can do in our town. | ☐ | ☐ | ☐ |

You can visit _____ .

You _____ .

| • describe things I can see and hear. | ☐ | ☐ | ☐ |

I can see _____ from my bedroom window.

When I wake up, I can hear _____ .

| • tell people what they must and mustn't do. | ☐ | ☐ | ☐ |

You must finish this. = _____ *(in my language)*

You mustn't go.   = _____

Don't interrupt!   = _____

Be quiet!   = _____

KEY WORDS

Abilities

play the piano _____ _____

dive _____ _____

_____ _____

_____ _____

_____ _____

Places in a town

shopping centre _____ _____

street _____ _____

_____ _____

_____ _____

_____ _____

Unit 8 was

interesting ☐   quite interesting ☐   not very interesting ☐

9 At the moment

1 Word work *Watching football*

Put the letters in the right order and write the words.

1 There's a football __match__ on TV. (*camht*)

2 It's the World Cup _____ . (*linaF*)

3 Two _____ people are watching the match. (*libinol*)

4 At the moment the _____ is 2–1 to Brazil. (*resco*)

5 I'm _____ Brazil. (*protguspin*)

6 So I'm wearing a green and yellow _____ . (*crafs*)

7 Italy have got another _____ . (*algo*)

8 It's 2 _____ now. (*lal*)

2 Reading *Football in England*

Read the text. Then match the words in **A** with the words in **B** and make sentences.

F ootball is England's national sport. There's the Premier League, and then three other leagues.

Manchester United, Arsenal and Liverpool are famous teams. They play in the Premier League. Every Saturday at least 700,000 people go to professional football matches in England. About 15% of the fans are women.

A lot of people watch football on television too. When there's an important European match (for example, Manchester United v Real Madrid or Arsenal v Juventus), nearly 20 million people watch the match on TV.

	P	W	D	L	Pts
Arsenal	38	25	8	5	83
Manchester Utd	38	23	9	6	78
Chelsea	38	21	6	11	69
Liverpool	38	19	10	9	67
Newcastle	38	18	10	10	64
Blackburn	38	16	12	10	60

A

1 England's national sport
2 Liverpool and Arsenal
3 Manchester United
4 Every Saturday, about 100,000 women
5 They support
6 A lot of people don't go to the matches,
7 About 20 million people

B

a watch big European matches on TV.
b but they watch football on TV.
c is football.
d their favourite team.
e is a very famous club.
f are both in the Premier League.
g go to football matches.

1 _c_ 2 _____ 3 _____ 4 _____ 5 _____ 6 _____ 7 _____

3 Present continuous: spelling

Look at the spelling notes on page 142 in the Student's Book. Write the present continuous form of these verbs and put them in the right list.

> argue   have lunch   sit   draw
> sing   get up

eat
He's eating

----

swim
He's swimming

----

come
He's coming

----

4 Present continuous: affirmative (G) 4a

Complete the text. Use these verbs in the present continuous.

> sit   drink   ~~watch~~   wear   stand
> eat   support

It's Saturday afternoon. Ben and Lisa
¹ **are watching** a football match,
Exeter City v Cambridge United. They
² _____ their team, Exeter City.
They ³ _____ red and white
scarves. The score is 2 all. They
⁴ _____ next to a Cambridge
United fan. He ⁵ _____ a
sandwich and he ⁶ _____
a can of lemonade. Look! Exeter have got
a goal! Lisa and Ben are very happy.
'3–2! Come on, Exeter!' The Cambridge
fan isn't happy. Lisa ⁷ _____
on his foot!

5 Present continuous: (G) 4c, 4d, 14 questions

Make questions. Then match them with the answers in the box.

> Next to Ben.   The housework.   Rick.   Some fish.
> ~~I'm writing an email.~~   Because it's late.
> A programme about lions.   To the swimming pool.

1 what / you / do?   What are you doing?
   I'm writing an email.

2 who / you / phone?   _____

   _____

3 where / she / go?   _____

   _____

4 why / they / leave?   _____

   _____

5 where / Sarah / sit?   _____

   _____

6 what / they / watch?   _____

   _____

7 what / he / do?   _____

   _____

8 what / the cat / eat?   _____

   _____

6 Extension *Use your imagination*

You're doing this exercise at the moment, but imagine you're in another place. What are you doing there? Write at least four sentences.

I'm sitting in a plane. I'm going to …

----

1 Present continuous: affirmative and negative  4a, 4b

Say what the people are/aren't doing. For each picture, use both verbs
and one of the words/phrases in the box.

| ~~homework~~ music tennis the spider a drink in the car |

1 do / dream

She isn't doing her
homework. She's
dreaming.

2 read / look at

He _____

3 work / listen to

I _____

4 play / argue

They _____

5 run / have

She _____

6 play / sit

They _____

2 Present continuous: questions and short answers  4c, 4d

Make questions. Then match the questions with the answers.

1 Mum / do the shopping? Is Mum doing the shopping? _____   **a** Yes, it is.

2 you / tidy your room? _____   **b** Yes, they are.

3 I / dream? _____   **c** No, he isn't.

4 they / argue? _____   **d** ~~Yes, she is.~~

5 Jack / have his lunch? _____   **e** Yes, you are.

6 the film / start? _____   **f** No, I'm not.

1 d   **2** ___   **3** ___   **4** ___   **5** ___   **6** ___

3 Listening *What's happening?*

📻 Listen to the sounds and the things people are saying. Then answer the questions.

1 What are they doing? ....

   Are they shouting? ....

2 What's she doing? ....

   Is she singing? ....

3 What's he doing? ....

   Is he supporting Brazil? ....

4 What are they doing? ....

   Is Joe having toast? ....

4 Object pronouns Ⓖ➤ 25a, 25b

Complete the sentences with object pronouns.

1 I've got a problem. Can you help ......*me*...... ?

2 I'm looking for Sadie, but I can't find ....

3 I've got some new shoes, but I don't like ....

4 Rick and I are going to the cinema. Do you want to come with .... ?

5 Have you got my scarf? I can't find ....

6 Joe is with Sadie. He's talking to ....

7 I know .... You're my sister's friend.

8 I like Lisa, but she doesn't like ....

5 Position of object pronouns Ⓖ➤ 25c

Look at the words in brackets. Put them in the right order and make sentences.

1 That's Sarah. (I / her / like)

   I like her.

2 Listen! (aren't / me / listening / you / to)

   ....

3 Oh, Elizabeth! (you / love / I)

   ....

4 I can't see Joe. (see / can / him / you ?)

   ....

5 Wait a minute! (interrupt / me / don't !)

   ....

6 I don't like pizza. (eat / I / never / it)

   ....

6 Extension *Write a dialogue*

Read the conversation. Then write a similar conversation. You can talk about CDs, videos, books, posters, computer games, etc.

A: I've got two new CDs.
B: Can I listen to them?
A: Yes. I've got Shakira.
B: Oh, I like her.
A: And the new Robbie Williams CD.
B: Great! I like him too.

A: *I've got two new* ....

   ....

   ....

B: ....

   ....

   ....

A: ....

   ....

   ....

B: ....

   ....

   ....

A: ....

   ....

   ....

B: ....

   ....

Unit 9   53

1 Key vocabulary *Clothes*

Read the descriptions and complete the words.

1 You wear this on your head.   h _a_ _t_

2 You can take an umbrella or you can wear this.   r ___ ___ ___ ___ ___ ___

3 A girl can wear a skirt or these.   t ___ ___ ___ ___ ___ ___

4 You wear these on your hands.   g ___ ___ ___ ___ ___

5 A T-shirt is a sort of ....   t ___ ___

6 These are trousers. They're often blue.   j ___ ___ ___ ___

7 You wear these when it's sunny.   s ___ ___ ___ ___ ___ ___ ___ ___

8 You wear these on your feet under your shoes.   s ___ ___ ___ ___

9 You can wear a sweater under this.   j ___ ___ ___ ___ ___

10 And you can wear a jacket under this!   c ___ ___ ___

11 You wear these on your feet on the beach.   s ___ ___ ___ ___ ___ ___

12 A footballer wears these.   s ___ ___ ___ ___ ___

2 What's she wearing today?

Look at the picture of Fiona. Complete the two sentences.

a What's Fiona wearing today?

She _____

_____ .

b What does Fiona usually wear?

She _____

_____ .

3 Extension *Your clothes*

Look at the examples. Then write three sentences about you.

I'm wearing black trousers and a red top.
I don't usually wear a jacket.
I never wear sandals.

_I'm_ _____

_____ .

I don't _____

_____ .

I never _____

_____ .

Unit 9 Learning diary

Date _____

At the end of Unit 9 I can:

	Easy	Not bad	Difficult

- describe things happening now.   ☐ ☐ ☐

  I'm writing my Learning Diary. I'm sitting _____ .

- ask questions about things happening now.   ☐ ☐ ☐

  What _____ *the Kellys doing?*   *What* _____ *Sadie watching?*

- remember and use object pronouns.   ☐ ☐ ☐

Subject pronoun	Object pronoun
I	*me*
He	_____
She	_____
It	_____

Subject pronoun	Object pronoun
We	_____
You	_____
They	_____

I can't do this.   Can you help _____ *?*

This is my new bike.   Do you like _____ *?*

Where are Joe and Sadie?   I can't find _____ *.*

- describe what I'm wearing today.   ☐ ☐ ☐

  Today I'm wearing _____ .

KEY WORDS

Verbs	Football	Clothes		
shout	*goal*	*shorts*	_____	_____
_____	_____	_____	_____	_____
_____	_____	_____	_____	_____
_____	_____	_____	_____	_____

Unit 9 was

interesting ☐   quite interesting ☐   not very interesting ☐

10 Plans

1 Key vocabulary *Time expressions*

Complete the sentences. Use time expressions: *tomorrow, next week, tonight,* etc.

1 Today is June 26th. .... is June 27th.

2 This month is April. .... is May.

3 This year is 2020. .... is 2021.

4 Students in England go to school from Monday to Friday. They

don't go to school ....

5 The Eddie Murphy film is here for two weeks. Do you want to

go this week or .... ?

6 See you .... Come to my house after dinner.

2 Present continuous used for the future  4f

Sally's friends are all busy tonight. What are they doing? Use the verbs in the box.

| play   have   ~~have~~   go   watch |

Are you free tonight?
Sally

Can't see you tonight. Meal with family. Alice

1 *Alice is having a meal with her family.*

Party at Sam's house tonight. Sorry! Tom

2 ....

No! Arsenal v Real Madrid on TV. Danny

3 ....

Piano lesson this evening. Sorry! Anna

4 ....

Basketball at sports centre. Helen

5 ....

3 Present continuous with future time expressions

Put the words in the right order and make sentences.

1 university / sister / next / is / my / to / year / going

My sister is going to university next year.

2 volleyball / I'm / tonight / playing

....

....

3 going / school / I'm / to / tomorrow / not

....

....

4 at / this / are / evening / staying / you / home ?

....

....

5 my / I'm / weekend / grandparents / visiting / the / at

....

....

6 going / you / on / are / Saturday / shopping ?

....

....

4 Suggestions: *Shall we? / Why don't we? / Let's*  26

Look at the pictures and write the suggestions.

1 Shall _we go bowling?_

2 Why _____

3 Let's _____

4 Shall _____

5 Let's _____

6 Why _____

5 Dialogue completion *Tom's birthday party*

Complete the conversation. Write the letters a–f.

a Shall we have a party on Friday?
b Let's make a list.
c We're meeting him at the station on Saturday evening.
d Why don't we have it on Saturday?
e I don't want to have a party on Monday evening.
f ~~Shall we have a party?~~

TOM: It's my birthday next Monday.

AMY: Great! [1] f

TOM: Yes, but [2] _____ It's school the next day.

AMY: [3] _____

TOM: Yes, OK.

AMY: Hang on a minute! I can't come on Saturday!

TOM: Why not?

AMY: My dad's coming home from America. [4] _____

TOM: Oh. What are you doing on Friday evening?

AMY: Nothing. [5] _____

TOM: Yes, I think that's OK.

AMY: How many people do you want?

TOM: I'm not sure. [6] _____

6 Extension *Your arrangements*

What are you doing next Saturday and Sunday?
Write at least three things.

On Saturday morning I'm playing tennis.

_____

_____

_____

_____

_____

1 *going to* Ⓖ➤ 8

Look at the picture. What are the people going to do?

1 He **'s going to catch a bus to London** .

2 They _____ .

3 She _____ .

4 He _____ .

5 They _____ .

6 She _____ .

2 *going to*: negative Ⓖ➤ 8

What aren't they going to do? Write a negative sentence each time. Use the words in the box.

| see her friends | stay in England | ~~eat meat~~ | wear my raincoat | learn French | take any photos |

1 I'm going to be a vegetarian.

   I'm not going to eat meat.

2 We're going to buy some postcards.

   _____

3 Joe is going to learn Spanish at school.

   _____

4 Mel's grandparents are going to live in Australia.

   _____

5 Sadie is going to work this evening.

   _____

6 I'm going to take my umbrella.

   _____

3 *going to*: questions and short answers G→ 8

Put the words in the right order and make questions. Then look at the sentences in Exercise 2 and answer the questions.

1 Spanish / is / to / Joe / learn / going ?

Is Joe going to learn Spanish?
Yes, he is.

2 to / going / England / stay / are / in / Mel's grandparents ?

3 going / are / postcards / buy / they / any / to ?

4 this / friends / to / evening / going / see / is / Sadie / her ?

5 you / vegetarian / be / going / to / a / are ?

4 Listening *Jack's plans*

🔊 Listen to Jack's conversation with Sadie. Put a tick (✓) next to the things he's going to do in London. Put a cross (✗) next to the things he isn't going to do.

1 go to the Tower of London ....

2 visit the Natural History Museum ....

3 see the blue whale ....

4 see Buckingham Palace ....

5 look at the shops in Oxford Street ....

6 buy some jeans ....

7 eat at a restaurant ....

8 take some sandwiches ....

5 What's the reply?

Complete the conversations. Circle the right reply: a, b or c.

1 I'm going to wash the car.
a Sorry, I'm not free.
b I can't do it now.
c That's a good idea.

2 Are you free?
a Yes, please.
b What am I going to do?
c No, I'm busy.   .

3 I'm going to make the lunch today.
a That's nice.
b Pasta with mushrooms.
c Why don't we have lunch?

4 Come on! Hurry up!
a Hang on a minute.
b OK. See you on Saturday.
c Are you going to come?

5 Where's my mobile?
a I'm going to buy a new mobile.
b Here it is.
c Thanks. I'm going to phone my mother.

6 Extension *Your plans*

Imagine you're in London. What are you going to do? Write at least three things.

I'm going to take a lot of photographs.

Tower of London

Oxford Street

1 Key vocabulary *The weather*

The sentences are wrong! Look at the map and write correct sentences.

1 It's sunny in Manchester.

It's cloudy in Manchester.

2 It's snowing in London.

....

3 It's raining in Edinburgh.

....

4 It's foggy in Exeter.

....

5 It's windy in Birmingham.

....

6 It's cloudy in Leeds.

....

7 It's hot in Edinburgh.

....

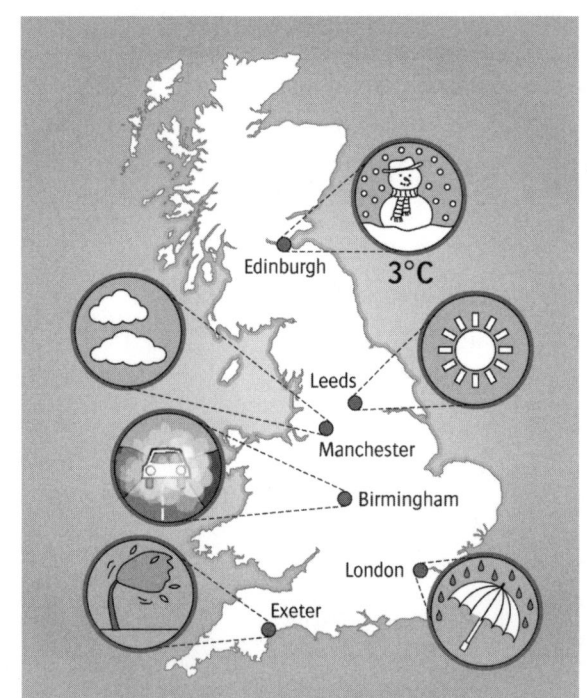

2 Reading *A postcard*

Read the postcard. Then complete the sentences. Circle a, b or c.

1 The postcard is from
   a Andy's mum.
   b Exeter.
   c New York.
2 It's to
   a Andy.
   b Louise.
   c New York.
3 The date is
   a 33°.
   b the first of July.
   c the tenth of July.
4 Louise is in
   a Exeter.
   b a plane.
   c New York.
5 It's
   a hot.
   b cold.
   c raining.
6 Louise is
   a wearing a short T-shirt.
   b going home on the 10th of July.
   c having a drink with Andy.

New York, 1st July

Dear Andy,

New York is an amazing city.
Mum and I are sitting in a café
in Times Square. We're having a
cold drink. I'm wearing shorts and
a T-shirt. It's 33°!

See you on the 10th.

Love,

Louise

Andy Garton
5 Bridge Street
Exeter EX3 9GY
UK

3 Extension *The weather and your plans*

Think of two sorts of weather. What are/aren't you going to do?

It's raining this morning. I'm going to / not going to ...

1 ....

   ....

2 ....

   ....

Unit 10 Learning diary

Date _____

At the end of Unit 10 I can:

	Easy	Not bad	Difficult
● talk about future arrangements.	☐	☐	☐

I'm _____ this evening.

We're _____ next Saturday.

	Easy	Not bad	Difficult
● make suggestions.	☐	☐	☐

Let's go home. = _____ *(in my language)*

Why don't we have lunch now? = _____

Shall we dance? = _____

	Easy	Not bad	Difficult
● accept or refuse an invitation.	☐	☐	☐

Yes, that's _____ . Thanks very much. See you on _____ .

Sorry, but I _____ . I'm busy.

	Easy	Not bad	Difficult
● talk about plans and intentions, using *going to*.	☐	☐	☐

I'm going to _____ .

	Easy	Not bad	Difficult
● ask about and describe the weather.	☐	☐	☐

What's the weather _____ ? It's hot. It's _____ .

KEY WORDS

Time expressions		**The weather**	
at the moment	_____	It's windy.	_____
this evening	_____	_____	_____
_____	_____	_____	_____
_____	_____	_____	_____
_____	_____	_____	_____

Unit 10 was

interesting ☐   quite interesting ☐   not very interesting ☐

About the past

1 Key vocabulary

Occupations

Match the letters in box A with the endings in box B and find eight occupations. Then write the occupations under the names.

(A) explore actr paint write act football ~~sing~~ scient

(B) -ess -r -er -or -ist

1 Pavarotti

   singer

2 Magellan

   ....

3 Van Gogh

   ....

4 J. K. Rowling

   ....

5 Russell Crowe

   ....

6 Galileo

   ....

7 Pelé

   ....

8 Marilyn Monroe

   ....

2 *was/were*: affirmative and negative (G) 3a, 3b

Where were they at nine o'clock this morning? Write questions and answers. Use *was, wasn't, were* or *weren't*.

1 A: *Where was* Dave?

   B: *He wasn't* at school. *He was* ....

2 A: .... Sarah?

   B: .... at school. ....

   ....

3 A: .... Pete and Sam?

   B: .... at school. They .... at ....

4 A: .... Mr and Mrs Carter?

   B: .... at work. ....

   ....

3 *was/were*: questions and short answers (G) 3c, 3d

Complete the dialogues. Use *was/wasn't* and *were/weren't*.

1 A: *Were* the Beatles scientists?

   B: No, *they weren't* . They .... pop stars.

2 A: .... Marilyn Monroe an explorer?

   B: No, ... She .... an American actress.

3 A: .... Galileo Italian?

   B: Yes, ... He .... born in Pisa.

4 A: .... Shakespeare and Roald Dahl painters?

   B: No, ... They .... writers.

5 A: .... you born in England?

   B: No, ... I .... born in ....

4 There was/were G→ 11d

Complete the poem. Use *There was* and *There were*. Can you think of a title for the poem?

Title: ....

a 🏠 in the 🌳 s   There was a house in the trees.

a 🐴 near the 🚪   There ....

a 💡 by the 🪟   There ....

a 🧀 on the floor   ....

two 🧤 s on the 🪑   ....

a black 🎩 in the hall   ....

three small 🔑 s in a silver ☕ ....

a silent 🕐 on the 🪟   ....

a 🖼 in my memory   ....

a happy, smiling 😊   ....

But ... empty 🪑 s in every room   But ....

And ... strange red 💡 s in 🪐   And ....

5 Listening *Were there any football fans?*

📻 Listen to the eight sounds. How many things can you remember? For each word write a true sentence. Use *There was a*, *There were some*, *There wasn't a* or *There weren't any*.

1 dog   There wasn't a dog. ....

2 horses   ....

3 train   ....

4 football fans ....

5 baby   ....

6 birds   ....

7 bass guitar ....

8 dolphins   ....

9 piano   ....

10 telephone ....

11 clock   ....

12 spaceship ....

6 Extension *Where were they?*

Think about the people at your home. Where were they at half past seven this morning? Where were you?

My sister was in the bathroom.

....

....

....

....

....

....

....

....

1 Past simple: regular verbs G→ 6a, 6e

Write the past simple form of the verbs. Then complete the sentences, using these past simple forms. Each verb goes in two sentences.

a live ___lived___

b study _____

c play _____

d save _____

e arrive _____

1 They _____ basketball yesterday.

2 She _____ in a small flat in New York.

3 I _____ all my money.

4 He _____ French at school.

5 They _____ in a taxi.

6 I _____ chemistry at university.

7 He _____ €100 in a week.

8 We _____ in an old house next to the river.

9 She _____ the piano when she was at school.

10 I _____ in London at ten o'clock.

2 Reading *The Beatles*

Read the article. There are 12 regular verbs in the past simple. Write a list.

The Beatles

The four Beatles were born in Liverpool. George Harrison was the lead guitarist. John Lennon was the rhythm guitarist. Paul McCartney played the bass guitar and Ringo Starr was the drummer. They started to play together at a Liverpool club, The Cavern. Their first record, *Love me do*, appeared in 1962. They stayed together for the next eight years.

When the Beatles arrived, there was a big change in the music industry. The group travelled all over the world. Their fans followed them in the street and waited for them at airports. People listened to their music in nearly every country in the world. Everyone loved them! Then in 1970 everything changed. They weren't happy together. Their musical interests were different and they wanted different things. It was the end of the Beatles.

But they were perhaps the greatest band in the history of popular music. A lot of people continue to buy their records today!

_____ ___played___ _____ _____ _____

_____ _____ _____ _____

_____ _____ _____ _____

3 True or false?

Look again at the article about the Beatles. Are these sentences true or false?

1 John Lennon was born in Liverpool. ___True.___

2 Ringo Starr wasn't the rhythm guitarist. _____

3 The band played at The Cavern, a club in Liverpool. _____

4 Their first record appeared in 1970. _____

5 After 1962 they stayed in Liverpool for eight years. _____

6 The Beatles changed the music industry. _____

7 People listened to their music all over the world. _____

8 Everyone liked them. _____

9 In 1970 their musical interests were the same. _____

10 The Beatles aren't popular today. _____

4 Making sentences

Match the words in A with the words in B and make sentences.

A	B
1 Zoologists	a she worked for a film company.
2 Jane Goodall was born	b to Africa.
3 She liked books	c in London.
4 She wanted	d study animals.
5 She wanted to be	e chimpanzees in Africa.
6 When she finished school,	f to work with animals.
7 She wanted to buy a ticket	g about animals.
8 She studied	h a zoologist.

1 _d_ 2 _____ 3 _____ 4 _____ 5 _____ 6 _____ 7 _____ 8 _____

5 Extension *Word work*

Match the words with the occupations.

> binoculars   concert   Shakespeare   jungle   ~~music~~   class   play
> students   voice   gorilla   film   lesson

singer	teacher	actor	zoologist
music	_____	_____	_____
_____	_____	_____	_____
_____	_____	_____	_____

1 Past simple: Wh- questions  6c, 6f

Put the words in the right order and make questions. Write the questions on the pictures.

she / who / phone / did ?

it / open / did / why / you ?

use / did / what / you ?

~~they / when / disappear / did ?~~

find / you / did / where / it ?

When did they disappear?

2 Make more questions  6c, 6f

Read the text. Then look at the answers and make eight questions with What/Where/Who/When.

Sadie started school when she was five. She liked the teachers, but she hated the food in the school canteen. She always preferred sandwiches.

Lessons started at nine o'clock. Sadie usually walked to school with Lisa and her mother. They usually arrived early and the girls played outside. School finished at half past three. When she was little, Sadie was very interested in animals and she wanted to be a zoologist.

1 A: When did Sadie start school?
   B: When she was five.

2 A: _____
   B: The teachers.

3 A: _____
   B: The food in the school canteen.

4 A: _____
   B: Sandwiches.

5 A: _____
   B: At nine o'clock.

6 A: _____
   B: Outside.

7 A: _____
   B: At half past three.

8 A: _____
   B: A zoologist.

3 Extension *Before you were famous!*

Think of a famous person. Write at least three questions about this person's life before he/she was famous. Choose from the verbs in the box.

| live | start | finish | like | prefer | hate | want | play | watch | be |

Where did you live before you were famous?

_____

_____

_____

_____

Unit 11 Learning diary

Date ....

At the end of Unit 11 I can:

	Easy	Not bad	Difficult
talk about people from the past.	☐	☐	☐

Picasso .... a painter.   The Beatles .... pop stars.

	Easy	Not bad	Difficult
spell the past simple form of these verbs.	☐	☐	☐

Present	Past simple	Present	Past simple	Present	Past simple
arrive	*arrived*	study	....	want	....
live	....	travel	*travelled*	watch	....
look	....	wait	....	work	*worked*
stop	....	walk	....		

	Easy	Not bad	Difficult
talk about things that happened in the past.	☐	☐	☐

When I was little, I wanted to be ....

When I was little, I ....

	Easy	Not bad	Difficult
ask questions about the past.	☐	☐	☐

.... you happy at primary school?   When .... you start school?

KEY WORDS

Occupations

pilot ....

....

....

....

Animals

gorilla ....

....

....

....

Unit 11 was

interesting ☐   quite interesting ☐   not very interesting ☐

12 Heroes

1 Reading *The Brooklyn Boys* G→ 6c, 6f

Read Sadie's article in the Westover School magazine. Then match the questions with the answers.

The amazing Brooklyn Boys were at the Westpoint Theatre in Exeter last night. There were six thousand people there. This was the group's first visit to England, and the fans loved them! The concert started at 8.30 and we enjoyed two hours of great music. Everyone wanted to hear the band's number one song, *You changed my world*. We waited for two hours!

Then the group announced the final number. 'And now we're going to sing our last song. Thank you, Exeter. You changed our world!' The fans danced and waved.

After the concert we waited outside the theatre, but we didn't get the Boys' autographs. They jumped into their car and disappeared!

Sadie Kelly

1 Were the Brooklyn Boys in London last night?	a Yes, she did.
2 Were there a lot of people at the concert?	b No, it didn't.
3 Did the concert start at half past eight?	c Yes, there were.
4 Did the concert finish at ten o'clock?	d No, she didn't.
5 Did the fans enjoy the concert?	e No, they weren't.
6 Did the Brooklyn Boys start with *You changed my world*?	f Yes, they did.
7 Did Sadie wait for the band after the concert?	g No, they didn't.
8 Did she get their autographs?	h Yes, it did.

1 _e_   2 ___   3 ___   4 ___   5 ___   6 ___   7 ___   8 ___

2 Past simple: negative G→ 6b

Are these sentences true or false? Correct the false sentences.

1 Picasso painted the Sistine Chapel in Rome.   *False. He didn't paint the Sistine Chapel.*

2 Jane Goodall studied chimpanzees.   *True.*

3 The Romans travelled in spaceships.   ___

4 John Lennon played for Manchester United.   ___

5 Bach and Mozart were writers.   ___

6 Marilyn Monroe lived in the USA.   ___

7 Enrique Iglesias was a member of the Beatles.   ___

8 The Aztecs used mobile phones.   ___

3 Past simple: questions Ⓖ➔ 6c, 6f

What did Alison do at the weekend? Look at the pictures and write the questions.

1 (stay) *Did you stay at home?*

Yes, I did.

2 (watch) _____

_____

Yes, I did.

3 (clean) _____

_____

No, I didn't.

4 (wash) _____

_____

Yes, I did.

5 (tidy) _____

_____

No, I didn't.

6 (phone) _____

_____

Yes, I did.

4 Word work *Time expressions*

Put the words in the right order and make sentences.

1 lessons / started / last / I / piano / year

I started piano lessons last year.

2 go / I / last / didn't / school / to / week

_____

3 the / didn't / at / football / I / play / weekend

_____

4 was / for / I / late / morning / school / yesterday

_____

5 you / night / home / did / at / last / stay ?

_____

5 Extension *Affirmative or negative?*

Are these sentences true or false? Correct the false sentences.

You played hockey at the weekend. *False. I didn't play hockey at the weekend.*

You travelled to London yesterday. _____

You were at school yesterday morning. _____

You didn't use your computer yesterday. _____

You weren't at school last week. _____

You watched television last night. _____

You studied English when you were three. _____

1 Past simple: irregular verbs G→ 7a

Find eight irregular past simple forms in the picture. Then write the infinitive of each verb.

left   leave

_____   _____

_____   _____

_____   _____

_____   _____

_____   _____

_____   _____

_____   _____

2 Irregular verbs: questions and answers G→ 7a, 7b

Luke went into town yesterday. Complete the questions and write the answers. Use these verbs.

| go | have | come home | speak | see | ~~leave~~ |

utleftroswenthkicamelewsawill grispoketynknewhyhadpimrate

1 What time *did he leave* ?

He left at half past one.

2 Where _____ ?

_____

3 What film _____ ?

_____

4 What _____ at the café?

_____

_____

5 What language _____ the woman _____ ?

_____

_____

6 What time _____ Luke _____ ?

_____

_____

3 Listening *Jack's holiday*

Sadie is talking to Jack about his holiday. Listen and circle the right answer: a, b or c.

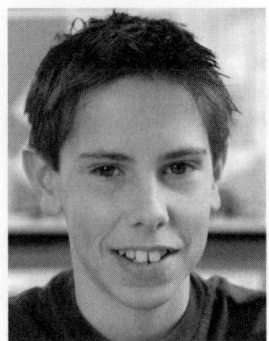

1 Where did Jack go?
   a He went to Italy.
   b He went to France.
   c With his family.

2 Was the weather nice?
   a Yes, it did.
   b Yes, it was.
   c No, it wasn't sunny.

3 Did they go to the Louvre?
   a It's a museum.
   b Yes, they did.
   c It's very famous.

4 Did he see the Eiffel Tower?
   a Yes, he went to the top.
   b No, he didn't.
   c Yes, it did.

5 What did he eat for lunch?
   a He usually ate a pizza.
   b He had bread and cheese.
   c It was OK.

6 Did he speak French?
   a Yes, about three words.
   b No, he didn't.
   c *Bonjour* and *Merci.*

4 Irregular verbs: affirmative and negative (G) → 7a, 7b

Complete the sentences. Use the right form of the verbs in brackets.

1 Lee had a party at the weekend. Barney .... **went** .... , but Mel .... because she had a cold. (*go*)

2 Sadie and Joe listened to a quiz on the radio last night, but Joe ...**didn't know**.... the answers. Sadie was pleased. She .... nearly all the answers. (*know*)

3 Lisa had lunch in the school canteen yesterday. She had fish and chips. She .... the chips, but she .... the fish because it was cold. (*eat*)

4 Barney danced with a girl called Monique, but he didn't talk to her because she .... English. She only .... French. (*speak*)

5 Jack went to town yesterday afternoon. He .... his friend Tom, but he .... Lisa because she was on holiday. (*see*)

6 Sadie played hockey for her school on Saturday. Her dad .... to the match, but her mum .... because she was at work. (*go*)

5 Extension *Where did you go?*

Think of your last holiday, or imagine a holiday, and answer the questions.

I went to Galicia.

1 Where did you go?

....

2 What was the weather like?

....

3 What did you see?

....

4 What did you do?

....

5 What did you eat?

....

1 Word work *A holiday crossword*

Read the clues and complete the crossword.

Across

1 You need a camera for these memories of your holiday. (6 letters)
4 You can go for a swim, and then you can sit here in the sun. (5)
6 Go on holiday to this country and learn American English! (3)
7 Is it hot? Are you thirsty? Buy a ...... of lemonade. (3)
8 If you don't like flying, you can go across the Atlantic on this. (4)
9 When English people go to France, they often catch this at Waterloo Station in London. (5)
10 Dolphins live here, and sharks! (3)
11 On holiday, you can ...... riding, swimming and surfing. (2)
12 If you're interested in the history of your holiday town, you can visit this. (6)
13 When they're on holiday, people like writing to their friends. So they buy these. (9)

Down

1 This takes you from London to New York in six hours. (5)
2 You must buy this before you go to the cinema or to a concert, and before you travel. (6)
3 When it's sunny, people often wear these. (10)
4 On the beach, you can play a lot of different games with this. (4)
5 If you don't want to stay in a hotel or an apartment, you can go ...... (7)
10 There's often a ...... near the campsite where you can buy food. (4)
12 When you're on holiday, this is very useful. It shows where places are. (3)

2 Past, present or future?

Put each sentence in the right list. Write a–j.

a ~~Sadie went to the Natural History Museum.~~
b Joe and Sadie live in Exeter.
c Kate is studying Biology at Bristol University.
d Lisa didn't speak to the Brooklyn Boys.
e Does Jack like animals?
f He's reading a book about a zoologist.
g Ben is going to buy a new skateboard.
h Lucy's parents had a baby.
i What did they call the new baby?
j Sadie is going to the judo club on Friday.

Past: ..*a*.. ....

Present: ....

Future: ....

3 Extension

Make more sentences

Write three more sentences about the people in the book.

Past: ....

....

....

Present: ....

....

....

Future: ....

....

....

Unit 12 Learning diary

Date _____

At the end of Unit 12 I can:

	Easy	Not bad	Difficult

- ask and answer questions about the past. ☐ ☐ ☐

  Did you _____ *yesterday?*

  Yes, I _____ .   *No, I* _____ .

- talk about things that didn't happen in the past. ☐ ☐ ☐

  When I was at primary school, we didn't study _____ .

  I didn't _____ *yesterday.*

- remember the past simple form of irregular verbs. ☐ ☐ ☐

Verb	Past simple
come	*came*
eat	_____
go	_____
have	_____

Verb	Past simple
know	_____
leave	_____
see	_____
speak	_____

- use irregular verbs to talk about the past. ☐ ☐ ☐

  I went _____ .

KEY WORDS

Time expressions

last year _____   _____

_____   _____

_____   _____

_____   _____

Holidays

pack _____   _____

_____   _____

_____   _____

_____   _____

Unit 12 was

interesting ☐   quite interesting ☐   not very interesting ☐

Grammar notes

Subject pronouns

1a

I	we
you	you
he she it	they

1b *You* is singular and plural.

Sadie and Joe, are you good at tennis?

They is masculine and feminine.

A: *Are the girls here?*

B: *Yes, they're in the living room.*

We always write *I* as a capital letter.

I'm Luigi and I'm Italian.

be: present simple

2a

AFFIRMATIVE	
Full forms	**Short forms**
I am He/She/It is We/You/They are	I'm He's/She's/It's We're/You're/They're

2b

NEGATIVE	
Full forms	**Short forms**
I am not He/She/It is not We/You/They are not	I'm not He/She/It isn't We/You/They aren't

2c

QUESTIONS	SHORT ANSWERS
Am I ...?	Yes, you are. No, you aren't.
Are you ...?	Yes, I am. No, I'm not.
Is he/she/it ...?	Yes, he/she/it is. No, he/she/it isn't.
Are we ...?	Yes, you are. No, you aren't.
Are you ...?	Yes, we are. No, we aren't.
Are they ...?	Yes, they are. No they aren't.

2d We use short forms (*I'm, he's,* etc.) when we speak and when we write emails or letters to friends. We use full forms when we write formal texts.

2e Note how we make questions.

Jack is English. ✗ → **Is Jack** English?

They're sisters. ✗ → **Are they** sisters?

2f We use the verb *be* in these expressions:

*I **am** twelve.*
*Sadie **is** hungry.*
*You **are** right.*

be: past simple

3a

AFFIRMATIVE	
I	was
He/She/It	was
We/You/They	were

3b

NEGATIVE	
I	wasn't (wasn't = was not)
He/She/It	wasn't
We/You/They	weren't (weren't = were not)

3c

QUESTIONS	SHORT ANSWERS
Was I ...?	Yes, you were. No, you weren't.
Were you ...? Was he/she/it ...?	Yes, I was. No, I wasn't. Yes, he/she/it was. No, he/she/it wasn't.
Were we ...?	Yes, you were. No, you weren't.
Were you ...?	Yes, we were. No, we weren't.
Were they ...?	Yes, they were. No, they weren't.

3d Note how we make questions.

Jack was happy. ✗ → **Was Jack** happy?

You were in London. ✗ → **Were you** in London?

Present continuous

4a

AFFIRMATIVE
I'm working. ('m = am)
He's/She's/It's working. ('s = is)
We're/You're/They're working. ('re = are)

4b

NEGATIVE
I'm not working.
He/She/It isn't working. (isn't = is not)
We/You/They aren't working. (aren't = are not)

4c

QUESTIONS	SHORT ANSWERS
Am I working?	Yes, you are. No, you aren't.
Are you working?	Yes, I am. No, I'm not.
Is he/she/it working?	Yes, he/she/it is. No, he/she/it isn't.
Are we working?	Yes, you are. No, you aren't.
Are you working?	Yes, we are. No, we aren't.
Are they working?	Yes, they are. No, they aren't.

4d Note how we make questions.

Mrs Kelly is working today.

Is Mrs Kelly working today?

They're working today.

Are they working today?

4e We use the present continuous to talk about actions that are in progress now, in the present.

Jack's watching television at the moment.
He isn't doing his homework.

A: *What are you doing?*
B: *I'm cleaning the elephant's teeth.*

4f We use the present continuous to talk about arrangements for the future.

A: *What are you doing tomorrow evening?*
B: *I'm watching the match on TV.*

Sadie isn't coming to the party next Saturday.

Present simple

5a

AFFIRMATIVE	
I	eat fish.
He/She/It	eats fish.
We/You/They	eat fish.

5b

NEGATIVE	
I	don't eat fish. (don't = do not)
He/She/It	doesn't eat fish. (doesn't = does not)
We/You/They	don't eat fish.

5c

QUESTIONS	SHORT ANSWERS
Do I eat fish?	Yes, you do. No, you don't.
Do you eat fish?	Yes, I do. No, I don't.
Does he/she/it eat fish?	Yes, he/she/it does. No, he/she/it doesn't.
Do we eat fish?	Yes, you do. No, you don't.
Do you eat fish?	Yes, we do. No, we don't.
Do they eat fish?	Yes, they do. No, they don't.

5d We use the present simple to talk about habits, regular activities and things that are generally true.

I play football every week.
My cousin lives in Peru.
Sadie doesn't eat meat.
Elephants don't play tennis.

5e In the third person singular (*he/she/it*), we add *s* (*he eats*). But:

- if a verb ends in *ch*, *sh*, *ss* or *o*, we add *es*.

  watch – he watches   *finish – it finishes*
  guess – he guesses   *go – she goes*
  do – he does

- if a verb ends in a consonant (*b, c, d, f, g,* etc.) + *y*, we change the *y* to *ies*.

  study – he studies   *carry – she carries*

5f Note how we make questions.

Jack eats fish.   *They eat meat.*

Does Jack eat fish?   **Do they eat** meat?

5g *Do, don't, does* and *doesn't* are parts of the present simple. But remember that *do* is also an ordinary verb.

Joe does his homework every evening.
I don't do judo.
What do you do at the weekend?

Past simple: regular verbs

6a

AFFIRMATIVE	
I/He/She/It/ We/You/They	worked.

6b

NEGATIVE	
I/He/She/It/ We/You/They	didn't work. (didn't = did not)

6c

QUESTIONS	SHORT ANSWERS
Did I work?	Yes, you did. No, you didn't.
Did you work?	Yes, I did. No, I didn't.
Did he/she/it work?	Yes, he/she/it did. No, he/she/it didn't.
Did we work?	Yes, you did. No, you didn't.
Did you work?	Yes, we did. No, we didn't.
Did they work?	Yes, they did. No, they didn't.

6d The past simple has the same form for all persons (*I, you, he, she, it, we, they*).

6e To form the past simple of regular verbs:

- we add *ed* to the infinitive.

    work – work**ed**   watch – watch**ed**
    play – play**ed**   listen – listen**ed**

- with verbs ending in *e*, we add *d*.

    live – live**d**   arrive – arrive**d**   close – close**d**
    like – like**d**   die – die**d**

- with short verbs ending in 1 vowel + 1 consonant, we double the final consonant and add *ed*. We do the same with all verbs ending in vowel + *l*.

    stop – sto**pped**   travel – trave**lled**

- with verbs ending in a consonant (*b, c, d, f, g*, etc.) + *y*, we change the *y* to *ied*.

    try – tr**ied**   study – stud**ied**   carry – carr**ied**

6f Note how we make questions.

Mrs Kelly worked yesterday.

Did Mrs Kelly work yesterday?

She worked yesterday.

Did she work yesterday?

6g We use the past simple to talk about actions in the past.

*We **didn't play** football yesterday. We **played** volleyball.*

A: **Did** Columbus **discover** Australia?
B: *No, he **didn't**.*

Past simple: irregular verbs

7a Irregular verbs do not have the usual *ed* ending in the past simple.

*see – **saw**   go – **went***

Look at the list of irregular verbs on page 143 in the Student's Book.

7b Like regular verbs, these verbs use *did* in questions and *didn't* in the negative form.

A: *Was Lisa at school today?* **Did** you **see** her?
B: *No, I **didn't**.*

*Mr Kelly **didn't go** to work yesterday.*

going to

8 We use *am/is/are* + *going to* + infinitive to talk about plans for the future.

A: **Are you going to wash** your hair?
B: *Yes, I am.*

*My brother's **going to buy** a new bike.*
*We **aren't going to live** in America.*

Imperative

9a We use the imperative to give orders or instructions. The imperative has got the same form as the infinitive.

Open the door!   **Listen** to the story!   **Stop!**

9b We form the negative imperative with *don't* (*do not*) + infinitive.

Don't open the door!
Don't touch that elephant!

have got

10a

AFFIRMATIVE	
I	've got (= have got)
He/She/It	's got (= has got)
We/You/They	've got

10b

NEGATIVE	
I	haven't got (= have not got)
He/She/It	hasn't got (= has not got)
We/You/They	haven't got

10c

QUESTIONS	SHORT ANSWERS
Have I got ...?	Yes, you have. No, you haven't.
Have you got ...?	Yes, I have. No, I haven't.
Has he/she/it got ...?	Yes, he/she/it has. No, he/she/it hasn't.
Have we got ...?	Yes, you have. No, you haven't.
Have you got ...?	Yes, we have. No, we haven't.
Have they got ...?	Yes, they have. No, they haven't.

10d Note how we make questions.

Jack has got a bike.   You've got a problem.

Has Jack got a bike?   **Have you got** a problem?

10e We use *have got* to talk about:

- possessions: *I've got a bike.*
- appearance: *She's got blue eyes.*
- relationships: *Sophie **has got** a brother.*
- illnesses: *The elephant **has got** a headache.*

10f We use *have* (NOT ~~have got~~) to talk about activities and things we eat.

*I **have** breakfast at 7.30.*
*Sophie **is having** a shower.*
*Lisa always **has** eggs for breakfast.*

there is / there are

11a We use *there is* + a singular noun and *there are* + a plural noun to say that something exists.

***There's** a café in Mill Street.*
***There are** two cinemas.*

***There isn't** a swimming pool.*
***There aren't** any tennis courts.*

A: ***Is there** a film on television?*
B: *No, **there isn't**.*

A: ***Are there** any girls in the band?*
B: *Yes, **there are**.*

11b We use *there is* (NOT ~~there are~~) in a list if the first thing is singular.

***There's** a café, a supermarket and two cinemas in Mill Street.*

11c Note how we make questions.

There's a car outside.

***Is there** a car outside?*

There are two men at the door.

***Are there** two men at the door?*

11d We use *There was/wasn't* and *There were/weren't* in the past.

***There was** a concert last night.*

A: ***Were there** any buses yesterday?*
B: *No, **there weren't**.*

can

12a

AFFIRMATIVE	
I/He/She/It/ We/You/They	can come.

12b

NEGATIVE	
I/He/She/It/ We/You/They	can't come. (can't = cannot)

12c

QUESTIONS	SHORT ANSWERS
Can I come?	Yes, you can. No, you can't.
Can you come?	Yes, I can. No, I can't.
Can he/she/it come?	Yes, he/she/it can. No, he/she/it can't.
Can we come?	Yes, you can. No, you can't.
Can you come?	Yes, we can. No, we can't.
Can they come?	Yes, they can. No, they can't.

12d *Can* and *can't* have the same form for all persons. They go before the infinitive without *to*.

12e Note how we make questions.

Jack can swim.   He can see me.

Can Jack swim?   **Can he** see me?

12f We use *can/can't* to talk about:

- possibility: *Sadie **can** come to the party, but Mel **can't** come. She's ill.*
- permission: A: ***Can** I watch TV?*   B: *Yes, but you **can't** sit in my chair!*
- ability: *I **can** play the piano, but I **can't** play the guitar.*

12g We often use *can* with the verbs *see* and *hear*.

Listen! I **can hear** a noise. (NOT I ~~hear~~ a noise.)
Look! I **can see** a spider. (NOT I ~~see~~ a spider.)

must/mustn't

13a

AFFIRMATIVE	
I/He/She/It/ We/You/They	must stop.

13b

NEGATIVE	
I/He/She/It/ We/You/They	mustn't stop. (mustn't = must not)

13c *Must* and *mustn't* have the same form for all persons. They go before the infinitive without *to*.

13d We use *must/mustn't* to talk about obligation.

*It's late. You **must** get up.*
*You **mustn't** be rude!*
*I've got toothache. I **must** go to the dentist.*

Wh- questions

14 Note the meaning of these question words.

A: ***What's** your email address?*
B: *jack@line.co.uk*

A: ***Who** are your friends?*
B: *James and Tom.*

A: ***Where** are Sadie and Joe?*
B: *They're in the kitchen.*

A: ***How** do you spell your name?*
B: *M-I-C-H-A-E-L .*

A: ***When's** your birthday?*
B: *The fourth of May.*

A: ***Why** is the elephant scared?*
B: *Because there's a ghost.*

Articles: *a, an, some* and *the*

15a We use *a* before words that begin with a consonant (*b, c, d, f, g*, etc.), and *an* before the vowels *a, e, i* and *o*.

*It's **a** message in **a** bottle.*
***An** elephant is **an** animal.*

15b The plural of *a/an* is *some*. *Some* = an indefinite number of things or people.

*There are **some** crisps in the cupboard.*

But we don't use *some* when we mean things, animals or people <u>in general</u>.

I like crisps.

15c We use *a/an* + thing/person when we aren't saying <u>which</u> thing/person.

*I saw **a** film last night. (We don't know which film.)*

We use *the* + thing/person when we're talking about a particular thing/person.

***The** film was brilliant. (We know which film. It's a particular one.)*

15d We use *the* before singular and plural words.

*Where is **the** telephone?*
*Where are **the** eggs?*

this/these, that/those

16a We use *this* (singular) and *these* (plural) to talk about things or people that are close to us. We use *that* (singular) and *those* (plural) for things or people that are further away.

***This** isn't my bag. **That's** my bag over there.*

A: *Which shoes do you like?*
B: *I like **these**, but I don't like **those**.*

16b We can use *this/these* and *that/those* before a noun.

*I know **that** girl.*
***This** pizza's good!*

Plural nouns

17 To form the plural we add *s* to most nouns.

elephant – elephants   pizza – pizzas   day – days

But some nouns are different. Look at the spelling notes on page 142 in the Student's Book.

Countable and uncountable nouns

18a Countable nouns are things that we can count. They've got a plural form.

a car – two cars   a girl – three girls
a story – some stories

18b Uncountable nouns are things that we can't count. They don't have a plural form. We use *some/any* with these nouns (NOT *a/an*).

*I want some **information**. (NOT an information or informations)*

*Is there any **bread**? (NOT a bread or breads)*

*Let's listen to some **music**. (NOT a music or musics)*

18c Nouns can sometimes be countable or uncountable.

*Countable: Can I have **two coffees**, please? (= two cups of coffee)*

*Uncountable: We need **some coffee**.*

some and any

19a We use *some* and *any* to talk about an indefinite quantity or number.

19b We use *some* in affirmative sentences, and *any* in negative sentences and questions. We use them before plural countable nouns:

*I've got **some** sandwiches.*
*There aren't **any** trains today.*
*Do you know **any** English songs?*

and before uncountable nouns:

*I've got **some** money.   There isn't **any** pasta.*
*Have you got **any** paper?*

Possessive 's

20a We use *'s* to show that something belongs to someone. We add *'s* to a singular noun.

*John is **Sophie's** brother.*
*The **elephant's** ears are amazing.*

With two names, we add *'s* to the second name.

*Joe is Kate and **Sadie's** brother.*

20b With plural nouns ending in *s*, we only add an apostrophe (*'*).

*This is my **parents'** bedroom.*

But with irregular plural nouns, we add *'s*.

*Where are the **men's** toilets?*

Possessive adjectives

21a

I	my	we	our
he	his	you	your
she	her	they	their
It	its		

21b The form of *my, your, his, her*, etc. is the same before a singular or a plural noun.

*This is **my** sister.*
***My** sisters are called Emma and Jenny.*

21c Note the use of *his* and *her*.

*Joe and **his** sister Sadie (Joe → his)*
*Kate and **her** sister Sadie (Kate → her)*

21d We use *its* when the possessor is an animal or a thing.

Look at that elephant!
***Its** ears are amazing.*

Adjectives

22a We use adjectives (*big, difficult, happy, good*, etc.) to describe people and things.

22b The form of the adjective is the same with singular and plural nouns.

*Sadie is **tired**.   Lisa and Ben are.**tired**.*

22c Adjectives go before the noun.

*I've got **blue** eyes.   That's an **interesting** idea.*

22d We sometimes use these words before an adjective.

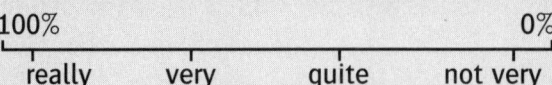

100%   0%
really   very   quite   not very

*She isn't **very** happy.*
*That film's **really** fantastic.*
*English is **quite** difficult, but **not very** difficult.*

Frequency adverbs

23a We use frequency adverbs to say how often something happens.

100% ─────────────────────────── 0%

always   usually   often   sometimes   never

23b Frequency adverbs usually go <u>before</u> the main verb.

*I **always** get up at 7 o'clock.*
*Do you **always** have cereal for breakfast?*
*Elephants don't **usually** eat spaghetti.*

23c But they go <u>after</u> the verb *be*.

*The bus is **sometimes** late.*
*Spiders aren't **usually** dangerous.*

Prepositions of place and time

24a We use prepositions of place to say where things are.

*Sadie is **in** her room.*
*There's a clock **above** the bed.*
*The shelves are **under** the window.*

24b *in*, *on* and *at* for place:

*He lives **in** Sydney, **in** Australia.*
*My books are **in** my bag.*
*Your camera's **on** the table.*
*There's a picture **on** the wall.*
*She's **at** the bus stop. He's **at** the cinema.*
*Sadie's **at** home. Mel's **at** school.*

24c *in*, *on* and *at* for time:

- *in* with months, years and parts of the day.

   *My birthday's **in** April.   He was born **in** 1993.*
   *She works **in** the morning/afternoon/evening.*
   *BUT He works **at** night.*

- *on* with days of the week and dates.

   *There's a concert **on** Friday.*
   *Her birthday's **on** 10th September.*

- *at* with clock times and particular times.

   *The concert starts **at** 7.30.*
   *I go home **at** lunchtime.*
   *I don't work **at** the weekend.*
   *He's in bed **at** the moment.*

Object pronouns

25a

I	me		we	us
he	him		you	you
she	her		they	them
it	it			

25b We use an object pronoun when it isn't necessary to repeat a noun.

*Can you see my glasses? I can't find **them**.*
(them = my glasses.)

25c We put object pronouns after the main verb or after a preposition.

Verb	Object pronoun
I love	**you**.
I don't like	**him**.

Verb	Preposition	Object pronoun
Don't talk	to	**her**!
I'm waiting	for	**them**.

*Where's my key? I can't find **it**.*
*That's Carlo, the new student. Do you know **him**?*

25d Don't forget the object pronoun!

*This is my new bike. Do you like **it**?*
(NOT ~~Do you like?~~)

A: *Have some ice cream.*
B: *Mmm! I like **it**. (NOT ~~I like.~~)*

Suggestions

26 To make suggestions, we can use:

- *Let's* + infinitive.

   A: *What are we going to do on Saturday?*
   B: ***Let's go** to the beach.*

- *Shall I / Shall we* + infinitive.

   A: *I'm hot.*   B: ***Shall I open** a window?*
   A: *I'm bored.*   B: ***Shall we go** to the cinema?*

- *Why don't we* + infinitive.

   A: *Where's Alderley?*
   B: *I don't know. **Why don't we look** at the map?*

An elephant never forgets!